PRAYER

HUMILITY

AND COMPASSION

תפלה

ענוה

רחמים

PRAYER

HUMILITY

AND COMPASSION

by SAMUEL H. DRESNER

wood engravings by ILYA SCHOR

PHILADELPHIA 5718–1957

THE JEWISH PUBLICATION SOCIETY OF AMERICA

to
RUTH

CONTENTS

CONTENTS

PROLOGUE

Where does God dwell?

This was the question with which the Rabbi of Kotzk surprised a number of learned men who happened to be visiting him.

They laughed: "What a thing to ask! Is it not written, 'The whole world is full of his glory'?"

Then he answered his own question:

"God dwells wherever man lets him in."

God's glory does fill the world, it is true; but just as the radiance of the sun, reaching everywhere, can be closed off by the palm of a hand before the face, so can the glory of God be shut out by the wall of the will before the soul.

God constantly pursues us, seeking us out in all places, at all times, yearning to enter our lives; and yet, in the weakness of folly, we flee him "down the nights and down the days . . . down the arches of the years . . . down the labyrinthine ways of [our] own mind."[1] God wants to enter our lives, but time and again we shut him out, closing the door on the divine.

Through the ages God has pursued man—sometimes drawing close; but, more often than not, unable to overtake him, forbidden to enter the portals of his heart and mind because of obstacles man himself has set in the way. Paganism, materialism and humanism have played their historic roles. In our own time, we, too, have erected barriers to God. Our understandable, but often uncritical infatuation with the amazing achievements of natural science have led many to conclude that only that exists which can be seen or touched or measured. And since God cannot be placed in a test tube or rendered visible by a microscope, He is thought to be a fantasy. With the advent of the atomic age, however, and the subsequent breakdown of scientific utopianism because of the unspeakable terror which now hovers on the horizons of society —threatening instant annihilation to millions, lingering death for millions more, and almost complete destruction to our entire civilization—such misconceptions about the role of science, after almost a century of unques-

12

tioned sovereignty, seem at last overthrown. Indeed, the scientists themselves, for they best see the fearful alternatives, now cry out most loudly for a spiritual source beyond science to check it, control it, and guide it.

But removing the barrier of science has not, *ipso facto*, made room for the reality of God. God's existence is not often denied today. There is too much concern for ultimate problems, too much disillusionment over false promises, too little confidence in the autonomous will of mortal man, and too much evidence of what a world without God, a people without God, and a man without God would be like. Still, admitting God's *existence in our world* is not the same as admitting his *reality in our lives.* For another barrier to God has been raised, perhaps even stronger than the first, and particularly prevalent among intellectuals who are exposed to the regnant rationalism which still rules at many centers of higher learning. This is the tendency to think of God as a hypothesis or concept, as some manner of force or process, ideal or idea. God exists in this sense, and He is no fantasy, but He exists only in a remote sort of way. He is the God of Aristotle, the Prime Mover, who created the world, gave it a push and then let it spin on without caring where it went or what happened to its creatures. To the philosopher, God may be a supposition or even a process which can be fitted securely into the pigeon-hole of some well-reasoned system; but whatever His role may be, He is surely not a God who wishes to enter the life of man.

"The God of the philosophers is all indifference, too sublime to possess a heart or to cast a glance at our world. His wisdom consists in being conscious of Himself and oblivious to the world. In contrast, the God of the prophets is all concern, too merciful to remain aloof from His creation. He not only rules the world in the majesty of His might: He is personally concerned and even stirred by the conduct and fate of man. 'His mercy is upon all His works.' "[2]

More than a century ago, during the so-called Period of "Enlightenment" of East-European Jewry, many Jews came in contact for the first time with the literature and philosophy of the West. Once one such "enlightened" young man was reading a book by a German thinker which, systematically and precisely, proved the existence and nature of God. Impressed by the brilliant display of logic, he hurried to a pious, old Jew, told him of the book and proceeded to recite at great length, syllogism by syllogism and detail by detail, the proof of God. When he had finished his recitation, the old man, deep in thought, looked at him for a while. "If God is, indeed, what you proved him to be," he finally said, "I would not believe in Him!"

The living God is more than any proof can provide.

Less than a century ago in the university city of Marburg, while the world-renowned professor of philosophy, Hermann Cohen, leader of the neo-Kantian school of thought and one of the most distinguished exponents of the rationalist movement, was taking his daily afternoon walk in the lovely park for which the city was noted, he met one of his students, a young Jew raised in the traditional piety of Polish Jewry, who had come to Marburg to study and to imbibe the great philosopher's wisdom of the western world. The teacher had noticed the pupil in class because of the seriousness which marked his face and the rapt attention with which he listened to the brilliant lectures of his professor, drinking in—but at the same time weighing—each of his words. Making the unusual gesture of stopping, Cohen extended greetings and asked the young student with the serious face and the searching eyes what he thought of the lectures just finished on the "idea" of God. The young student was taken aback. That he should be asked such a personal question by the great man, the author of heavy tomes and the idol of hundreds of scholars, seemed most unusual. Unable at once to answer, he lowered his eyes. Then he gathered strength, the years of his youth welling up within him, giving him courage. Finally he raised his eyes and spoke in a clear voice:

"Herr professor, everything which you have said is brilliant and most profound. It may even

15

be true. But one thing I should like to know: what remains of the *Ribono shel Olom?*"*

At these words, at least so it is told, Hermann Cohen burst into tears.

The living God is more than any mind can manufacture.

Pascal, one of the great mathematicians of history, sewed into the lining of the coat that he wore until the day of his death a scrap of paper upon which were written words that have a peculiar relevance today: "Not the God of the philosophers, but the God of Abraham, Isaac, and Jacob." Not the remote, aloof God of the philosophers—the concept or process, hypothesis or idea of which they speak—who cares little for man and his concerns, but the God of our fathers: the God who discovered Abraham in Ur of the Chaldees and tried him at Moriah, who appeared with a blessing in the night to Isaac at Beer-Sheba, who struggled in the darkness with Jacob in Beth El that he might be changed into Israel; the God who spoke of freedom to Moses at the burning bush, of holiness to Isaiah in the Temple of Jesrusalem, of justice to Amos in the bleak wilderness near Tekoa, of judgment to Jeremiah and of forgiveness to Hosea; the God who struck awe into the heart of Job and love and fear into the soul of David, who taught Elijah to be afraid of no man and gave Nathan the

* Master of the world.

16

strength to fight kings; who humbled Hillel and turned Akiba to repentance, who shone upon Maimonides, illumined Elijah of Vilna and set a ladder in the earth that the Baal Shem might ascend into heaven, the God who reveals His will, who hears our prayers, who shares our suffering, who has mercy on those in need and compassion for those in privation, who searches after righteous people and seeks out the upright man.

Pascal's phrase has a fiery meaning for our time, when many of us have been beguiled by the thinking of recent centuries which has attempted to remove God from the crucible of life and fit Him into the neat pages of a book, setting Him apart from the unavoidable decisions that confront us daily, the inescapable anxieties and worries, joys and comforts which are the lot of humankind, transforming Him into the objective and the debatable, the abstract and often irrelevant. We stand in need, not of the philosophers' God about which one reads in the cool of his study or speculates upon in the leisure of the lecture hall, who is distant and unconcerned, remote and unapproachable; but of our father's God who pursues us "down the nights and down the days . . . down the arches of the years," seeking to enter our hearts and souls and lives.

PRAYER

"Lord, I have called daily upon Thee,
I have stretched out my hand unto Thee."

"The Holy One, blessed be He, hovers over
the lips of men, when they utter words of
prayer with fear and love, to kiss them."

PRAYER AND THE MODERN AGE

Prayer does not come easily to us of the present generation. Faith in God and converse with Him was the natural heritage of our forefathers whose hearts were illumined by His presence as each day they stood before Him morning and evening in love and fear, His words on their tongues, His dreams in their minds, His visions haunting their souls. But both God and worship are strange to us. Prayer, unhappily, is not something this generation has inherited. It is something which we or our parents considered expendable, something to be cast off like so much excess baggage. It must be discovered all over again, and rediscovery is not easy. Many of us seem quite satisfied to do without it. We have replaced it with other activities and remedies; with the psychiatrist and the television program. Why bother with prayer at all? Yet the absence of worship has not nourished the soul of modern man. His spiritual health is not robust. He complains of fears and anxieties that rob him of the joys of his days and the quiet repose of his nights.

21

Neither his wisdom and power nor his gadgets and wealth have brought him the happiness he has expected.

In abandoning prayer, we have cut ourselves off from the source of our being, have grown weak and shallow, sick and ugly. We silently grope for what we have lost, not knowing what it is that we have lost or what it is that we grope for. We secretly yearn for what we have forsaken, not understanding what it is we have forsaken or what it is that we yearn for.

And God? He waits. The One before whom we may cast all our thoughts, pour out all our tears and reveal all our needs, our strength in time of suffering, our vantage point to view the world, our guide to daily living, the perfect shelter for our soul—He stands ready to receive us as peace, power and infinite mercy.

MAN: A PRAYING ANIMAL

Prayer makes us human. This is the bold claim of religion. To understand prayer we must first understand man. What is man, this strange creature who has set himself astride all history, seeking to conquer the world; who, endeavoring to fathom the secrets of the universe, finds—after weighing the wind, counting the raindrops, capturing the sunlight and exploding the atom into untold energy—that he himself, his heart and mind and soul, is the most hidden and unfathomable secret of them all?

From the point of view of science man is so

much chemistry. Some years ago a chemist published the following analysis: The average man is five feet eight inches in height, weighs one hundred and sixty pounds, contains enough fat to make seven pounds of soap, enough iron to make a nail of medium size, enough sugar to fill a bowl, enough lime to whitewash a chicken-coop, enough phosphorus to make two thousand match-tips, enough potassium to explode a toy cannon, plus a small amount of sulphur. This, he said, is man. On the current market, he would be worth about four and a half dollars.

From the point of view of the Bible, how different is man! He is, to be sure, a part of nature and to that extent he can be analyzed and examined by the scientist in the same manner as any other piece of matter. He is born and he dies, he eats and procreates, is composed of flesh and blood, and is subject to disease and pain. He was created out of the dust of the earth. But the Bible asserts that he is also a part of the world of spirit, that God, who fashioned him from the dust of the earth, placed within him an immortal soul. Man is like a cord tied at two ends: bound to the earth through his body and to heaven through his soul. He is partly animal through the physical aspect of his being and partly angel through the spiritual aspect of his being. He is mortal yet immortal, transient yet eternal, filled at once with misery and grandeur. Like Jacob's ladder, he is fixed into the ground beneath, but his head touches the sky above.

What is it that binds man to the earth? His body. What is it that joins man to heaven? His soul. How does he sustain his body? By the food he eats. How does he preserve his soul? Through the prayer he offers. Prayer is to the soul what food is to the body. It provides the sustenance necessary for the life of the spirit.

Science says man is an animal. Philosophy agrees, adding that he is an animal with a mind. The Bible, however, claims more: that man is an animal with a soul. Not just an animal, nor a thinking animal, but a *praying* animal. It is in his ability to commune with God that man's uniqueness and his essence lies. Man may best be described as an animal that prays, and by whose prayers animal is transformed to angel, flesh to spirit, earth to heaven. The life of man is determined by his worship. A man *is* what he prays.

Prayer teaches us that man cannot live without something more than man. "As a tree torn from the soil, as a river separated from its source, the human soul wanes when detached from what is greater than itself."[1] Man is part beast and part angel. When he forgets the angel within him and the heavens above him, his spirit grows sick, for there is nothing to draw him upward and beyond, nothing to carry him forward toward old and new ideals, and he slips downward into the clutches of what

24

lies hidden in the depths of his soul. Man is not an autonomous being who created himself and sprang to full stature from the dust of the earth, independent of all else, reliant on no one else. In the pride of his achievements, when he parades the fascinating gadgets he has fashioned and beholds the tinsel splendor of his skyscrapers and his factories, he may well believe that he needs no guide, no will, no source beyond the genius of himself. But when this happens—and that it does happen we know from what our own eyes have seen—then man becomes something less than man, his spirit withers and the beast within him, taking courage, gains in the struggle for the mastery of his soul. For we are attached at the root of our soul to One who is greater than all our wisdom, all our genius, all our creations, and from whose grace the power of life flows. Forget that source, cut ourselves loose from that guidance, and we begin to decay, grow weak in heart and are overcome by all the terrors of history. It is prayer that joins us to that source, draws upon that guidance, makes firm the root of our soul in the Root of all souls.

"Prayer is our attachment to the utmost. Without God in sight, we are like scattered rungs of a broken ladder. To pray is to become a ladder on which thoughts mount to God, to join the movement to Him which surges throughout the entire universe."[2]

Prayer is thus a meeting of the infinite and

25

finite, a joining of that which is born and dies with Him who lives on forever, a coming together of the holy within man with the holy beyond man, of creature and Creator, communion between man and God. Still, it is difficult for the mind to comprehend, a miracle too magnificent to accept. How strange and how unbelievable this meeting and joining and communion! What is man that Thou, O Lord of all creation, art mindful of him, and the son of man that Thou, O Eternal One, thinkest of him?

> *Man's origin is dust and he returneth to the dust. He obtaineth his bread by the peril of his life; he is like a fragile potsherd, as the grass that withereth, as the flower that fadeth, as the fleeting shadow, as a passing cloud, as the wind that bloweth, as the floating dust, yea, and as a dream that vanisheth.*[3]

Yet God does think of man. The fate of man weighs heavy upon the mind of God. He created man and has not cast him off to fend for himself, leaving him to rely on his own frail resources. He cares for man and is concerned for his destiny. He will not desert him. Indeed, He has made man a little lower than the angels. He has granted him the supreme gift: communion with God through prayer. For the finite and the infinite to meet, for the soul encased in a fragile piece of dust, precarious

26

and perishable, passing and provisional, to join
with the Soul of all souls, seems impossible,
incredible, beyond the wildest range of the
imagination. Yet this is precisely the claim of
prayer. "*I have taken upon me to speak unto
the Lord,*" said Abraham, "*who am but dust
and ashes.*"[4]

The Rabbi of Zans told the following story.
"People come to me who ride to market every
day of the week. One such man approached me
and cried: 'My dear rabbi! I haven't gotten
anything out of life. All week I get out of one
wagon and into another. Yet when a man stops
to think that he is permitted to pray to God
Himself, he lacks nothing at all in the world.' "

There was a man who felt this truth so deeply
that he composed a special prayer, found in the
large prayer books of our forefathers, which
gives thanks for the miracle of worship. It is, in
fact, a prayer for prayer.

"Who am I that I should be worthy to pray
before the Holy One blessed be He? For He is
the great and awesome Lord, while I am but
a sinful creature who brings shame to His great
Name through my wicked deeds. Yea, I am
only flesh and blood, dust and ashes, unworthy
even to bring from my lips His great, mighty and
awesome Name, how much the less to pray
before Him and utter His great Name many
times. Woe is me, for how shall I raise my face
to stand before the great and revered King of
all kings, the Holy One blessed be He, Cause

27

of all causes, Source of all sources? And yet, I do so, because of the tenderness and mercy He pours forth upon His creatures. For He desires the prayers and the supplications of His servants, as it is written, 'The Lord is nigh unto all those who call upon Him, unto all who call upon Him in truth. He will fulfill the desires of those who fear Him: He will hearken to their pleas and will save them. To Him who hearkens to prayer, all flesh shall turn.' "[5]

GOD AND THE WORLD

"If 'prayer is the expression of the sense of being at home in the universe,' then the Psalmist who exclaimed, 'I am a stranger on earth, hide not Thy commandments from me' (119: 19), was a person who grievously misunderstood the nature of prayer. Throughout many centuries of Jewish history the true motivation for prayer was not 'the sense of being at home in the universe' but the sense of *not* being at home in the universe. We could not but experience anxiety and spiritual homelessness in the sight of so much suffering and evil, in the countless examples of failure to live up to the will of God. That experience gained in intensity by the soul-stirring awareness that God Himself was not at home in the universe, where His will is defied, where His kingship is denied. *The Shekhinah is in exile*, the world is corrupt, *the universe itself is not at home. . . .*

"To pray, then, means to bring God back

28

into the world, to establish His kingship, to let His glory prevail. This is why in the greatest moments of our lives, on the Days of Awe, we cry out of the depth of our disconcerted souls, a prayer of redemption:

> And so, Lord our God, grant Thy awe to all Thy works, and Thy dread to all Thou hast created, that all Thy works may fear Thee, and all who have been created prostrate themselves before Thee, and all form one union to do Thy will with a whole heart.

"Great is the power of prayer. For to worship is to expand the presence of God in the world. God is transcendent, but our worship makes Him immanent. This is implied in the idea that God is in need of man: His being immanent depends upon us."[6] This is the paradox: that He who is the Lord of all creation, infinite and perfect, above all worlds and beyond all thought, is at the same time as close to man as an ear to a mouth; that He who makes His abode in the highest heavens also dwells among men. Therefore the Psalmist said, *Thou art holy, O Thou who dwellest amidst the prayers of Israel.* Even though Thou art holy, O Lord, through the wonder of prayer we have the power to bring Thy holiness down from heaven to earth, among men and women and nations, among the affairs of mankind. "When we say *Blessed be He*, we extend His glory, we bestow

His spirit upon this world. *Yithgadal Ve-yith-kadash: Magnified and sanctified be God's great name throughout the world. . . . May there be more of God in this world.*"[7]

SURRENDERING TO THE STILLNESS

"Prayer is one of those things which stand on the heights of the world and at which men mock." How precious and how sweet is prayer, and how rarely is it found! The soft whisper of worship is silenced by the gallop of the herd in search of power and glory and knowledge. True prayer has almost disappeared in our time. Samuel Goldwyn, the Hollywood producer, once remarked that he would like to make a movie which would begin with an earthquake—and then work up to a climax. Prayer is the opposite of such a movie.

So filled with noise, confusion and excitement are many of our lives that there is little room for prayer. If in the midst of our rushing about we were suddenly stopped and asked our destination, we should be embarrassed. Continually absorbed with one thing or another, often involved in a hundred inconsequentials, most of us are fearful of our solitude and are almost afraid to be alone with nothing but ourselves. Yet Rabbi Moshe Leib of Sassov once said that a "human being who has not a single hour for his own, each day, is not a human being."

When I was a student in New York and lived

in the vicinity of Harlem, I often took long walks in that bustling neighborhood full of a thousand surprises. One afternoon, while strolling down its busiest thoroughfare which resounded with all the clatter of which New York can boast, I was attracted by an unusual sign located among the names of doctors and their office numbers: *"Center for Silence. Open from Twelve to Two, Come Up and Sit in Silence."* I was curious and decided to investigate. On the second floor of the building I found a room where men and women, tired of the Harlem jungle, might in silence cast off the stridor of the street and find the peace they so desperately needed. That room was an outpost of repose, a haven of serenity in a world gone mad. Elijah the prophet would have appreciated that room, for Elijah knew the secret of silence and understood its purpose.

> *"And behold, the Lord passed by, and a great and strong wind rent the mountains, and broke in pieces the rocks before the Lord; but the Lord was not in the wind. After the wind an earthquake; but the Lord was not in the earthquake. After the earthquake, a fire; but the Lord was not in the fire. And after the fire there came a still small voice. And it was so, when Elijah heard it, that he wrapped his face in his mantle and went out and stood in the entrance of the cave."*[8]

31

Elijah was not alone in that cave. All of us are there with him. We spend the days of our years in that cave. That cave is our world. Some hear only the wind and the earthquake and the rending of rocks; others, possessing the prophet's discerning wisdom of spirit, understand that amidst the silence there is a sound, and within the quiet there is a voice.

Prayer is a surrendering to the stillness that surrounds us, a withdrawal from the marketplace, the honking of horns, the television set, the innumerable diversions and attractions which modern living thrusts upon us, and a yielding to the quiet that is everywhere. For there is another world about and within us which we neither see nor touch, a world which is as real as the flowers we smell or the ground we walk upon, as the mountains we behold or the rock we lean against. There is One who at all times and in all places speaks to us with love and guidance and concern; but He speaks in a tone barely audible and we must clear away the din of daily living and open our ears to hear Him.

"To the philosopher God is an *object*, to men at prayer He is the *subject*. Their aim is not to possess Him as a concept of knowledge, to be informed about Him, as if He were a fact among facts. What they crave for is to be wholly possessed by Him, to be an object of His knowledge and to sense it. The task is not to know the unknown, but to be penetrated

32

with it. *Not to know*, but *to be known* to Him, to expose ourselves to Him rather than Him to us; not to judge and to assert but to listen and to be judged by Him."[9]

Prayer implies another dimension of reality beyond the human to which man attempts to relate himself. In prayer we open ourselves to God; we lower the barriers and let Him come into our lives. "Prayer is an invitation to God to intervene in our lives, not only through our walking in His ways, but through his entering into our ways."[10] In prayer God enters the life of man. We do not know God in prayer, but make ourselves known to Him. We do not discover Him, but expose ourselves to His constant yearning to be with us. As on the first warm, sunny day of spring, after a long, cold dreary winter, we feel the warmth of the sun against our skin, soothing and comforting it, so in prayer we get out of ourselves into the constant healing rays of God's presence which seek to stream through the fabric of our being.

"Thou shalt love the Lord thy God with all thy heart, with all thy soul and with all thy might; and these words, which I command thee this day shall be upon thy heart."[11] The verse does not say *"in thy heart,"* as one might expect. For the heart of man is usually shut fast, so that the word of God cannot enter and must remain suspended upon the heart of man. But there are rare and holy hours, hours of prayer, when man surrenders himself to the stillness of

33

the universe, and then the heart opens—and God's words sink deep into it.

FORMS OF PRAYER

"Prayer appears in history in an astonishing multiplicity of forms; as the calm collectedness of a devout individual soul, and as the ceremonial liturgy of a great congregation; as an original creation of a religious genius, and as an imitation on the part of a simple, average religious person; as the spontaneous expression of upspringing religious experiences, and as the mechanical recitation of an incomprehensible formula; as bliss and ecstasy of heart, and as painful fulfillment of the law; as the involuntary discharge of an overwhelming emotion, and as the voluntary concentration on a religious object; as loud shouting and crying, and as still, silent absorption; as artistic poetry, and as stammering speech; as the flight of the spirit to the supreme Light, and as a cry out of the deep distress of the heart; as joyous thanksgiving and ecstatic praise, and as humble supplication for forgiveness and compassion; as a childlike entreaty for life, health, and happiness, and as an earnest desire for power in the moral struggle for existence; as a simple petition for daily bread, and as an all-consuming yearning for God Himself; as a selfish wish, and as unselfish solicitude for a brother; as wild cursing and vengeful thirst, and as heroic intercession for personal enemies and persecutors; as a stormy clamor

34

and demand, and as joyful renunciation and holy serenity; as a desire to change God's will and make it chime with our petty wishes, and as a self-forgetting vision of and surrender to the Highest Good; as the timid entreaty of the sinner before a stern judge, and as the trustful talk of a child with a kind father; as swelling phrases of politeness and flattery before an unapproachable King, and as a free outpouring in the presence of a Friend who cares."[12]

OUT OF WONDER

Prayer often arises out of a sense of awe and wonder. "In his prayer a man should know that the Shekhinah* is before him."[13] Above the holy ark in most synagogues are inscribed the words, "Know before Whom thou standest." The knowledge that we stand in His presence and that His ineffable glory is before us, fashions a mood of worship out of neutral moments and evokes words of prayer from a slumbering soul. Man responds to God's presence and God's goodness in prayer. The sense of awe and wonder at His reality and His deeds fills the heart with that praise and thankfulness and adoration which we call worship.

We stand in God's presence at all times. His works are ever before us.

Thou compassest my path and my lying down, Thou art acquainted with all my ways.

* Divine Presence.

35

For there is not a word in my tongue,
But lo, O Lord, Thou knowest it altogether.
Whither shall I go from Thy spirit?
Or whither shall I flee from Thy presence?
If I ascend up into heaven, Thou art there;
If I make my bed in the nether world, behold
    Thou art there.
If I take the wings of the morning,
And dwell in the uttermost parts of the sea;
Even there would Thy hand lead me,
And Thy right hand would hold me.
And if I say: "Surely the darkness shall envelope
    me.
And the light about me shall be night;"
Even the night shineth as the day;
The darkness is even as the light.[14]

It is the loss of the sense of wonder in our
own time that has impoverished our ability to
pray. We look at the world as if God did not
exist, as if we owed God nothing for our lives
and dreams, our hopes and joys, as if all these
were coming to us as our right. Modern man
has learned too easily to take things for granted.
Yet who are we to have been given the blessing
of a star's radiance, a child's kiss, a tree's shade,
a mother's devotion, the rain which comes, the
wind that blows, the falling leaves, the chang-
ing seasons, the days and nights that never fail,
the love that flows from man to man? A favorite
parable of the Baal Shem was of a fiddler who
played so sweetly that all who heard him began

to dance. Then a deaf man, who knew nothing of music, happened along. To him all he saw seemed the action of madmen, senseless and in bad taste.

The music is playing, but some do not hear; wonders are before us, but some do not look. "Alas for those who see but do not know what they see, that stand but do not know upon what they stand."[15]

The world is full of God's wonders. The heavens declare the glory of God and the firmament showeth His handiwork. All of nature testifies to His glory. O Lord, our Lord, how glorious is Thy name in all the earth whose majesty is rehearsed above the heavens, who does great things past finding out, marvelous things without number. Wondrous are Thy works, and that my soul knoweth exceedingly. Who is like unto Thee, O Lord, majestic in holiness, working wonders? How can we fail to rejoice in Thy glory, O Lord? Yet man sees many things but does not observe them; his ears are open, but he does not hear. O, would that he might stand still, for a moment of quiet, and consider the wondrous works of God! Lift up your eyes on high, O man, and see who created all these. Open Thou mine eyes, O Lord, that I may behold wondrous things out of Thy Torah. O give thanks to Him who alone does great wonders.

Such are the words of Scripture.

In worship Israel responds:

"We give thanks unto Thee . . . for Thy miracles which are daily with us and for Thy wonders . . . which are wrought at all times, evening, morn and noon. . . ."[16]

Miracles have always played a central role in religious debate. Pious men cite them as incontrovertible proof of the truth of their religions; skeptics deny their possibility. But while both the skeptic and the orthodox debate the miracles of yore in the isolation of their studies, a miracle—just as glorious, just as breathtaking, just as surpassing as any of the ancient ones—takes place in our world every day. But we, in the folly of our blindness, and the frenzy of our haste, every day ignore it.

What is that miracle?

The setting of the sun!

But the prayer book has not forgotten. It is alert to the wonders of God's world. And the Jew, who turns aside from his cares when the shadows lengthen and night falls, opens his *siddur* and prays the evening service, is reminded, each and every day:

Praised be Thou, O Lord our God ruler of the universe, who with Thy word bringest on the evening twilight, and with Thy wisdom openest the gates of the heavens.[17]

Prayer teaches us to be aware of the miracles of life, never to forget nor to take them for granted.

"The words of the Midrash," writes Hayim

Greenberg, "sound constantly in my ears: 'The wicked is as one dead, even in his lifetime, for he sees the sun rise without reciting the blessing "Thou who formest light"; he sees its setting without reciting the blessing "Who bringest on the evening twilight"; he eats and drinks without thanking God. But the righteous thank God for whatever they eat and drink and see and hear.' What does the Midrash mean? Surely the mere recitation of 'Thou who formest Light,' and 'Who bringest on the evening twilight' cannot infuse life into the righteous any more than the failure to recite them can deprive the wicked of life so that he should be 'as one dead.' The meaning of the Midrash is that the wicked is so dead spiritually that he cannot feel the need to recite the bendiction and take delight in so doing; he is so dead that he cannot sense the mystery in the rising and setting of the sun, in the piece of bread that he eats and the measure of water that he drinks; he is unaware of the eternal link between these things and the whole of existence and with God who dwells in this existence. The wicked is as one dead because he has lost the sense of wonder, because he views the appearances of eternity as mundane happenings."[18]

"The sense for the miracles which are daily with us, the sense for the continual marvels, is a source of prayer. There is no worship, no music, no love, if we take for granted the blessings or defeats of living. No routine of the social, physical or physiological order must dull our sense of surprise at the fact that there *is* a social, a physical, or a physiological order. We are trained in maintaining our sense of wonder by uttering a prayer before the enjoyment of food. Each time we are about to drink a glass of water, we remind ourselves of the eternal mystery of creation, 'Blessed be Thou . . . by whose word all things came into being.' A trivial act and a reference to the supreme miracle."[19]

So it is that in prayer we praise. Standing in His presence and opening our eyes to His wonders both in the world of nature and the world of man, viewing the majesty of the heavens and the innocence of a child, knowing the fragrance of a flower and the warmth of a friend's hand, gazing upon a distant mountain and a deed of kindness, watching a bird in its flight and a baby smile, experiencing the cool breeze of a summer wind and the warm love of one's beloved, feeling all the beauty and goodness and grandeur of the world—we give praise and thanksgiving unto Him who formed the earth and breathed the breath of life into man, by whose word all was brought forth, Who looked out upon creation and said it was good, even very good, and by whose goodness and mercy the miracles of creation are renewed each day.

Bless the Lord Oh my soul.
O Lord my God Thou art very great,
Thou art clothed with honour and majesty.

O Lord how manifold are Thy works
In wisdom hast Thou made them all.
O Lord how excellent is Thy name in all the
   earth.[20]

OUT OF LOVE

Prayer not only arises out of our sense of
wonder or awe, but out of our feeling of love as
well. "One verse says: *Thou shalt fear the Lord
Thy God*, and one verse says: *Thou shalt love
the Lord Thy God*. So man should act both
from fear and from love."[21] To fear God is to
stand in reverence; to love God is to move
towards His embrace.

Within the human soul is a yearning for
God, a movement that cannot be halted, a song
that cannot be stilled, the feeling that all our
strength, all our devotion, all our life are His,
that we and all we have belong to Him, that
our one desire is to enter into His arms and
find rest within the shelter of His wings. It is as
though the soul—having been born in a secure
home, nurtured with infinite care and tenderness, surrounded by endless love and affection,
and having wandered far into a distant land
filled with danger and evil and strange creatures
who harm and humiliate and hamper—cease-
lessly dreams of its first home and anxiously
yearns to return once again to it. So it is that
man seeks to flee into the arms of God, as a
child its mother, a lover his beloved, a friend
his trusted companion. For the Lord is mother,

beloved, comrade—and more. And the desire for God is more. "*Whom have I in heaven but Thee? And beside Thee I desire none upon earth. . . . They that go far from Thee shall perish . . . But as for me the nearness of God is my good.*"[22] "I do not want Your heaven, nor am I afraid of Your hell," said one of the hasidic saints; "I want only You."

Many of us have been taught that God cannot hear our prayers, since He is only a process, a force or an idea. We do not pray to Him—that would be sheer magic—but to the "good within us" or for the purpose of identifying ourselves with the group. It is understandable that after the rise of the modern scientific attitude, a revulsion set in against the primitive notion that prayer could alter the course of nature. One might, as a matter of fact, have expected such modernists to have eliminated prayer as a vestige of ancient superstition. The fact that they have not done so, but have endeavored to retain prayer—albeit in an emasculated fashion, by making it an address to one's better self rather than to God, a soliloquy rather than a dialogue, or a means of group identification—is high tribute to the inexorable need for prayer. It proves that there is a flame in the soul which cannot be quenched, a deep longing which stems from our love for God Himself—the living God, not an idea or process—which we are afraid and sometimes even ashamed to express.

There are so many misconceptions of prayer and so many obstacles, inner as well as outer, that we sometimes wonder why men pray at all. Perhaps the best answer was given by William James. "We pray," he said, "because we cannot help praying." Yet with our mental inhibitions, our modern manners and mores, we children of the twentieth century have grown too sophisticated to declare openly what we feel, to ask freely what we crave for, to utter with our tongue what lies hidden within our heart.

The soul cries out silently within us, declaring that we have talked enough about God, saying we believe in Him, discussing His Bible, His temple, His people, His world, His creed, His deeds. What about God Himself? Unless we have Him we have nothing. All our talk about Him, all our interest in Him, all our activities for Him are in vain. The greatest danger to religion is a religion which is secondhand, hearsay, where God is a "rumor fostered by dogmas."[23] Man longs for the living God, the great, mighty and revered One, the Lord of justice and the Father of compassion, who seeks to touch our souls with His holiness and kindle our spirits with His flame. The coals of love have not gone out; they still glow within each breast and wait only to be kindled upon the altar of prayer.

As the hart panteth after the waterbrooks,
So panteth my soul after Thee, O Lord.
My soul thirsteth for God, for the living God.[24]

O God, Thou art my God.
Early will I seek Thee;
My soul thirsts for Thee;
My flesh faints for Thee.
As in a dry and weary land where no water is,
I have searched for Thee in the sanctuary,
To behold Thy grandeur and Thy glory;
For Thy lovingkindness is better than life.[25]

OUT OF NEED

In prayer we petition: "O Lord make my business prosper; grant me recovery from my illness; give me relief from my pain; save my child from its misery; spare my husband's life; deliver me from the trouble which surrounds me." These are prayers of petition; in them we ask God to do something for us. It is only natural that we bring before the Lord our cares, concerns and needs. But "words do not stem the flood, nor does meditation banish the storm. Prayer never entwines directly with the chain of physical cause and effect; the spiritual does not interfere with the natural order of things."[26] "The essence of prayer is not man's influence upon God, but the mysterious contact which comes to pass between the finite and infinite Spirit."[27] Prayer is not a liturgical slot machine, in which we insert the coin of words and from which miracles jump forth at the press of a lever. In Greek "to pray" means "to wish," and in German, "to beg," but the central meaning

44

of Jewish prayer is not *to get something*, but
to be with Someone.

Our needs and worries, our concerns and
petitions, serve to initiate prayer and to bring
us into contact with God. They begin a process
which leads beyond the narrow interests of the
ego and into the realms of the infinite. The
real issue of prayer is not the self; indeed, it is
precisely in that moment when we *forget* the
self, our worries and needs, and become aware
of His presence, when in the act of asking for
ourselves we suddenly realize that we stand
before Him who fashioned us in love, watches
over us in compassion and ever seeks to enter
our lives, that all our private concerns seem
petty and trite. It is in that very moment that
our petition turns into prayer.

A man suffering with cancer may be led to
prayer. It is doubtful whether there is any relation between the words he utters for recovery
and the physical condition of the cells of his
body. But in devout prayer for physical recovery, he may for the first time open his heart to
God, feel His presence close, gain a new
strength and a new understanding of life's
meaning and purpose which he never knew
before. He may better withstand his illness and,
perhaps, learn a lesson from it.

Prayer cannot cure cancer, but it can help
us endure the suffering and it can help us turn
that suffering into insight.

A man who has failed in business may turn

to God in prayer. It is doubtful whether there is any direct relation between the words he prays and his economic condition. His petition will not fill his ledger with orders, nor his pockets with gold. But, again, in the fervent prayer that he not be brought to poverty, which arises out of his fear and anxiety, he may for the first time open his heart to God in humility and contrition, step aside from the world that was always too much with him, and become aware of another world, the world of the spirit. He feels God's presence and God's love, gains a new insight into life and acquires a new set of standards. He is able to see his vocation in a new perspective. Life is not for the purpose of acquiring wealth, but of serving God, whose stewards we are of whatever we possess. Business is not an end in itself, but only a means to higher ends. Thus he may emerge from his trouble with new strength and a new way.

Prayer cannot bring economic success, but it can help us survive failure and emerge wiser than we were before.

There are numerous prayers of petition in our prayer books. They are, we should note, however, put into the plural tense, so that we are taught to pray as a member of the community of Israel: "Hear our cry; forgive us; heal us; blow the great horn of our freedom." It is as if we were being told that we should really not pray for our own needs; that is not true prayer; often it is only selfish concern. Our prayers should be for His will to be done, for our wills to bend to His, for Him to enter our hearts. Yet, we are human and have human needs and desires that stir us deeply. And it is easier for us to ask for our own needs than for God's, for our will to be done rather than for His. Therefore, we may ask and we may petition. But we are not to ask for ourselves. We are to ask for our people and all mankind. And, then, in the midst of this asking and petitioning, we will come to understand that all our petitions, all our requests, all our pleas are only so that we might turn away from the world and stand before Him for a moment to know His love and strength; that His presence might be made manifest to us.

What begins with man's request ends with God's presence; what starts in the narrowness of the ego, emerges into the wide expanse of humanity; what originates in concern for the self becomes a concern for others and concern for God's concern; what commences in petition concludes as prayer.

"O God," wrote Bachya ibn Pakuda, a medieval thinker, "I stand before Thee, knowing all my deficiencies, and overwhelmed by Thy greatness and majesty; but Thou hast commanded me to pray to Thee, and hast suffered me to offer homage to Thine exalted Name according to the measure of my knowledge, and to make my humble submission unto Thee. Thou knowest best what is for my good. If I recite my wants, it is not to remind Thee of them, but only so that I may understand better how great is my dependence upon Thee. If, then, I ask Thee for the things that make not for my well-being, it is because I am ignorant; Thy choice is better than mine, and I submit myself to Thine unalterable decrees and Thy supreme direction."

WHAT TO CHERISH

Many are the paths which stretch before man. Each beckons him on, promises him that along its trail there are no deep pits to leap, no sharp boulders to climb, no swift rapids to cross, no dangers to be encountered. There is only a smooth, straight, swift road through life which can be traversed with a minimum of effort and a maximum of reward. Many are the standards which call out to man: accept us as your guide, live your life according to our counsel. Ruthlessness, selfishness, hardheartedness and deceit present themselves to us as the best and often the only way for achieving success in daily living. The life histories of any number of successful men seem to teach the same lesson. And who is to say that the best of us, after listening long enough and resisting with less and less vigor, may not in the end accept these values? At such a time the power of prayer can manifest itself.

In prayer we learn what to cherish. Prayer trains us to distinguish between the crooked and the straight, the darkness and the light, the false and the true, the right and the wrong, the path of God and that of Satan. The mind of the man at prayer meets the imperishable ideals of faith: peace and righteousness, mercy and holiness, justice and humility, love for the Torah, love for God and love for our fellow man. In the midst of worldly living, when our thoughts are scattered and our wills are weak, the Hebrew prayer book keeps before our eyes what might otherwise so easily be forgotten: *That you go not about after your own desires and your fancies after which you go astray: that you remember and do all My commandments and be holy unto your God.*[28] Prayers are signposts along the way, visible even in the fog, pointing in the right direction and reminding us what to remember.

STRENGTH FOR LIFE

In prayer we find strength for life. Temptation and passion, as well as irritation and torment, plague us constantly. Each day has its ordeals, and at times we wonder if we shall survive them. There comes a time in the life of each of us when everything crumbles at our feet; all the supports upon which we were accustomed to lean—wealth, possessions, friends, relatives—slip away into nothingness. When death takes a loved one, a yawning void opens in our lives that nothing seems to fill; the petty thoughts we have, the small talk we indulge in, the day to day routine of our habits—sleeping and eating, working and playing—suddenly appear cheap and unworthy. When failure is our lot and that upon which we had set our hearts, for which we had labored long and hoped for fervently, is lost to us—a love unrequited, a child turned wayward, a friend untrue, a promise broken—despair settles upon us. When without warning calamity comes—a business disaster, a painful illness, a consuming disease, a broken limb, a broken heart—the dark mantle of melancholy casts its pall over us and we are enveloped by a cloud of meaninglessness and bitterness and foreboding which threatens to take the taste of the joy of living from our mouths. Our days are filled with gloom and we begin to sink beyond the helpful words of friends and the bright light of the sun into the dark misery of our own heart, alone and forsaken, broken and defeated.

At times of death and failure and despair, when we can turn to no one else—for no one else understands, no one else seems to care, no one else will really listen—we turn to God. Prayer breaks forth. And comfort comes.

Save me, O God;
For the waters are come in even unto the soul.
I am sunk in deep mire where there is no
standing;
I am come into deep waters, and the flood over-
whelmeth me.

I am weary with my crying; my throat is dried;
My eyes fail while I wait for my God . . .

Hear my cry, O God;
Attend unto my prayer.
From the end of the earth will I call unto Thee,
    when my heart fainteth;
Lead me to the rock that is too high for me.
For Thou hast been a refuge for me,
A tower of strength in the face of the enemy.

I will dwell in Thy tent forever;
I will take refuge in the covert of Thy wings.[29]

HIS JUDGMENT

In prayer we open ourselves in self-surrender to God's judgment. We often repress our real thoughts and what is truly in our hearts. Pent up in little chambers and firmly bolted against the curious gaze of the world are the actual hopes and fears of our lives. Much pain and suffering come from the hiding of our real selves in the subconscious of our souls when we refuse to share our problems with others for fear that they may think less of us. Many a psychiatrist's couch has held the twisted, nerve-wracked soul of one who could bear the burden of his secrets no longer, so that at last it burst the evenness of his mind. In prayer we find a release for what is stored within us.

What we can say to no human being we can say to Him; what we must hide from the eyes

51

of man we can reveal to God; what has burned within us during hours of anguish can be brought forth and laid before the altar of His presence. In the quiet of our room we can be alone with Him who fills the world. There we can feel that a friend is near who will understand all we say, listen to all our words, be patient with all our complaints. He is a friend who has endless time, endless compassion and endless strength. All our fears and regrets, our crimes and jealousies, our hatreds and loves, our bitternesses and joys, our secret hopes and bitter disappointments, our fervent wishes and anxieties, our dreams and disappointments, our past failures, present sins and future apprehensions pour forth in an overflowing stream of honesty and frankness from a heart opened to Him. A confession of sin and an expression of confidence, a surrendering to God of our deepest feelings, an offering up before the Lord, in fear and trembling and hope, the story of our lives.

And then, having opened our hearts to Him and having revealed the tale of our days, we stand still and wait for Him to gather up the scattered words of our devotion, to enter the gate we have opened for Him and to make His presence felt that His judgment might prevail. It is as though we cried: "Here am I. And this is the record of my days. Look into my hopes and regrets."[30]

*Search me, O God, and know my heart;
try me and know my thoughts; and see if
there be any wickedness in me, and lead
me in the way everlasting.*[31]

PEACE

In prayer we find peace. Out of the struggle
and the complaint which pours forth from a
heart of anguish, out of the fear of what to-
morrow may bring and what yesterday has
brought—all of which we offer up to God in
the torrent of words and thoughts and feelings
that tumble from the heart of a troubled man—
there comes the sweet feeling of inner peace,
trust and resignation. We possess the knowledge that we are not forsaken and that man is
not alone in the world. We have the certainty
that there is One who takes us up into His
bosom, wipes away our tears, caresses our brow
and draws us close in love and compassion,
One who loves us freely and endlessly. "However high He be above His world, let a man
but enter a Synagogue, stand behind a pillar
and pray in a whisper, and the Holy One
Blessed be He hearkens to His prayer. Can there
be a God nearer than this, One Who is close
to His creatures as a mouth to an ear?"[32] The
knowledge that God is near and that God
loves us banishes all fear, extinguishes all
worry. His presence casts a cloak of security
about us, calming all anxiety, soothing all pain,
comforting all sorrow. When the Baal Shem's

father was about to die, he took his young son into his arms and said: "My time has come and it has not been permitted me to rear you to manhood. But, dear son, remember all your days that God is with you and around you and beside you whenever you call upon Him, and that because of this, you need fear nothing in all the world."

INWARD DEVOTION

Perhaps the most difficult act to imitate is prayer, for in prayer we learn to tell the truth. *"The Lord does not see as man sees; for man looks on the outward appearance, but the Lord looks on the heart."*[33] We cannot lie when speaking to God. The falsehoods we utter (with small pangs of conscience) each day to a multitude of persons somehow stick to our tongue and numb our lips when we try to say them in prayer. What can be said to man cannot so easily be said to God. There are things which we desire greatly, but about which we feel uncomfortable in prayer. Pride, knowledge, charm, achievements, cleverness are stripped from us when we stand before the Lord of all creation. The sentences we utter are not sufficient; the words which spring from our lips do not say enough. Prayer without inwardness is like the body without the soul. "My words fly up, my thoughts remain below." The words of prayer are sometimes less important than what is left over after they have passed our lips, what we are unable to express. (Perhaps this explains the importance of music to worship.) "God desires the heart."[34] Our inner feeling, *kavvanah* (inwardness, devotion), not a rote recital of memorized phrases, is what God wants in our prayer. As with an arrow, the farther one stretches the bow backward, the greater the strength which is given to the arrow and the farther it flies forward. So it is with the man at prayer. The deeper the prayer presses downward into the very depths of his heart—until the heart can no longer contain the prayer—the greater the force with which it overflows and bursts forth from the heart and the higher it ascends.

The ancient rabbis knew that worship was a matter of the heart:

"Scripture says, *To serve the Lord your God with all your heart* (Deut. 11.13). What is service with the heart? It is prayer. One must not stand up to pray except in a serious frame of mind. So the pious men of old used to wait an hour, and then pray, in order to direct their hearts to their Father in Heaven. Always let a man test himself: if he can direct his heart, let him pray; if he cannot, let him not pray. A man's prayer is not accepted unless he puts his heart in his hands, for prayer requires *kavvanah*. Thus a man must purify his heart before he prays. Let him cast his eyes downwards, but turn his heart upwards. Let him not recite his prayers as if he were reading a document, but a new prayer should be said each day. For if a man makes his prayer a fixed task he has not truly prayed. This refers to one whose prayer seems to him a burden, or one who is not able to add something new to it. God says to Israel, 'I bade you pray in the Synagogue in your city; but if you cannot pray there, pray in your field; and if you cannot pray there, pray on your bed; and if you cannot pray there, then meditate in your heart and be still.'"[35]

Once the Baal Shem stopped on the threshold of a House of Prayer and refused to go in. "I cannot go in," he said, "it is crowded with teachings and prayers from wall to wall and from floor to ceiling. How could there be room for me?" And when he saw that those around him were staring at him and did not know what he meant, he added: "The words from the lips of those whose teaching and praying does not come from hearts lifted unto heaven, cannot rise, but fill the house from wall to wall and from floor to ceiling."

With prayer, more than anything else perhaps, it is not the quantity which counts, the number of words or pages we recite, but the quality of the recital, the inner feeling we express.

A villager, who year after year prayed in the Baal Shem's House of Prayer during the Days of Awe, had a son who was dull-witted and could not learn to read the holy words. On these days his father did not take him to town

with him, because the boy did not understand
anything. But when he was thirteen and of age
according to the laws of God, his father took
him along on the Day of Atonement, for fear
the boy might eat on the fast-day simply because he knew no better.

Now the boy had a small whistle which he
always blew when he sat out in the fields to
herd the sheep and the calves. He had taken it

with him in the pocket of his coat and his father
had not noticed it. As the boy sat through
the Kol Nidre service and for the first time saw
people praying, he wanted to join them, but
he did not know how to read from the book,
as they were doing. In the morning the service
continued and the mood of the prayer created
an indescribable yearning in the boy. "Father,"
he said, "I have my little whistle with me. I

57

want to sing on it." The father was greatly perturbed and told him to do no such thing. The boy restrained himself. When the afternoon service began and the yearning came over him again, he said, "Father, do let me blow my little whistle." The father became angry and said, "Where did you put it?" And when the boy told him, he laid his hand on his pocket so that the boy could not take it out. Now *Neilah*, the final prayer, that prayer wherein Jews pour out their tired hearts to God in tears and joy before the closing of the gates, had begun. The boy, unable to restrain himself any longer, snatched his pocket away from his father's hand, took out the whistle and blew a shrill note. All were frightened and confused. But the Baal Shem went on with the prayers and later remarked that it was the boy's whistle which had lifted all their prayers to heaven.

OUTWARD OBSERVANCE

It is true that the essence of prayer is not to be found in the building we worship in, the books we worship from, or the formalism which accompanies it. The essence of prayer is not to be found in what goes on *about* us, but in what goes on *within* the heart and soul of man. Yet this view may lead us to think that we should abandon the established forms of worship, cut ourselves adrift from hallowed traditions, and pray only at certain random moments when we feel an inner need, a sweep of emotion, a pang of contrition, a fullness of thanksgiving. The Torah, however, speaks clearly on this subject, and wisely too. Jewish prayer requires regular worship, the constant, day by day contact with the words of the prayer book, with other men at prayer and with our Father in heaven—even if we ourselves are not moved to prayer every day. The truth tradition teaches us is that *we learn to pray through prayer itself.*

There is a story about a small town, far off from the main roads of the land. In the town were all the necessary municipal institutions: a bathhouse, a cemetery, a hospital and a law-court. And there were all sorts of craftsmen: tailors, shoemakers, carpenters and masons. One trade, however, was lacking; there was no watchmaker. In the course of years, many of the clocks became so annoyingly inaccurate that their owners decided to ignore them altogether. Others, however, maintained that as long as the clocks ran they should not be abandoned. So they wound their clocks, even though they knew that they were not accurate. One day, when the news spread through the town that a watchmaker had arrived, everyone rushed to him with his clock. But the only clocks he could repair were those that had been kept running. The abandoned clocks had grown too rusty.[36]

THOSE WHO PRAY: THE SAINTS

When the Jewish contributions to civilization
are enumerated, mention is usually made of
Einstein's theory of relativity or Freud's theory
of psychoanalysis. But prayer is rarely, if ever,
alluded to. Yet western man, whatever his land
and whatever his religion, has adopted the Jewish way of prayer. Israel has taught most of the
world how to pray. The liturgy of both Church
and Mosque bears the mark of the Synagogue,
and the psalms in a thousand different languages are the golden links in that great chain
which binds man to God.

The Baal Shem once taught his disciples
through a parable:

A great and mighty king issued a proclama-
tion that on a certain festive day all requests
would be granted. Some asked for gold, others
for land, still others for weapons of war. Each
wish was fulfilled. But there was one man wiser
than the others. His request, he said, was only
that he be permitted to enter the palace and
speak in person with his royal highness, the
king, three times a day. His request found more

favor in the eyes of the king than all the others.

So it is with the King of kings. The nations, too, have made their requests. Some have asked for gold, others for great stretches of land, still others for powerful armies. But Israel, wanting none of these things, asked only to visit the King of kings, the Holy One blessed be He, in His palace three times a day, morning, afternoon and evening, in prayer.

The Jews have no powerful armies, no mighty empires, no vast treasuries of wealth. They are a small and poor people, scattered amidst the nations. Yet a power immeasurable girds and preserves them. It was the mystery of prayer which awoke in the hearts of patriarchs, prophets and psalmists thousands of years ago and which they held more precious than empires or wealth and tended and watched over in Tabernacle and Temple until the wonder of worship was revealed to them, that has been their stay from generation to generation. Is anything more dear to man whether in privation or joy than that he can open his heart to the One who ever listens and who ever speaks courage and truth and goodness to that heart?

Let me relate several traditions regarding the Jewish saints to illustrate the role prayer played in their lives.

A hasidic rabbi, who was accustomed to delay his morning prayers several hours beyond

61

the regular time, was once asked what he did during those hours, for he could be seen up and about from early dawn.

"I pray," he replied, "that I may be able to pray."

It is told in the name of the Baal Shem that the saints of old used to meditate one hour before prayer and one hour after. During the hour before, they thought about the vanity of man and the glory of God. During the hour after, they dwelt upon the fact that they had not prayed as one should pray before a great king and that their prayers had achieved nothing at all.

"A man," said the Baal Shem, "must consider before he prays that he is prepared to offer his life during that prayer because of his glowing fervor. And, in truth, it is only because of the great lovingkindness of the Lord, may He be blessed, that we are given the strength to complete our prayers and still live."

Rabbi Levi Yitzhak of Berditshev was standing before the holy ark, leading the congregation in prayer when, all at once, overwhelmed by the endless sufferings of his people at the hands of nations in whose midst they dwelt, like Abraham daring to argue with the Almighty Himself, he halted the service, raised his eyes toward heaven and uttered a prayer of his own:

Good morning to You, Lord of the world!
I, Levi Yitzhak, son of Sarah of Berditshev,
   approach you with a legal matter concern-
   ing Your people of Israel.
What do You want of Israel?
It is always: Command the children of Israel!
It is always: Speak unto the children of Israel!
Merciful Father! How many peoples are there
   in the world?
Persians, Babylonians, Edomites!
The Russians—what do they say?
   Our emperor is the emperor!
The Germans—what do they say?
   Our kingdom is the kingdom!
The English—what do they say?
   Our kingdom is the kingdom!
But I, Levi Yitzhak, son of Sarah of Berdit-
   shev, say:
   Yiskadal Veyiskadash Shemay Rabo!
   Glorified and sanctified be His great Name!
And I, Levi Yitzhak, son of Sarah of Berdit-
   shev, say:
   I shall not go hence, nor budge from my
      place
   Until there be a finish
   Until there be an end
   Of the exile—
   Glorified and sanctified be His great Name!

Rabbi Mendel of Rymanov used to say that,
during the time he was reciting the *Amidah*,
all the people who had ever asked him to pray

to God in their behalf would pass through his mind.

Someone once asked him how that was possible, since there was surely not enough time. Rabbi Mendel replied: "The need of every single one leaves a trace in my heart. In the hour of prayer I open my heart and say: 'Lord of the world, read what is written here!' "

It is told of the Baal Shem that once, while in the midst of prayer, he began to reflect upon his life and found that he was not worthy of inheriting the Future World. Melancholy descended upon him. After a few moments, however, he said to himself:

"If I have within me the love of God, what need is there for a Future World?"

Then he continued to pray with great fervor.

The great mystic, Isaac Luria, was accustomed to say before each prayer: "Behold I acknowledge the commandment, *Thou shalt love thy neighbor as thyself*," for he desired to hold each man as dear to him as his own soul in order that his prayers might be in the name of all the people of Israel.

It was to the prayers of the children of Jacob, when saints such as these lived among them, that the words of the ancient rabbis refer: "The angel who is appointed over prayer waits until the Israelites in the last synagogue have finished their worship, and then he gathers up all the prayers of Israel, fashions a chaplet out of them and places it upon God's head."[37]

THOSE WHO PRAY: THE PEOPLE

The fact that in days gone by almost every Jew made prayer an integral part of his daily living can easily lead us to a romantic exaggeration of the role it played in the life of the people. We must beware of assuming that everyone prayed like the saints, that each silent devotion was a bridge to heaven. Undoubtedly in a culture where prayer, public and private, was part of the expected regimen of life, there must have been people who went through the motions of worship as many modern Americans go through the motions of friendship or charity without feeling the inward meaning. It is important, especially in view of the fact that we deplore our present prayerless state of mind, not to romanticize the past unduly. But if there is danger in romanticizing the past, there is also the danger of underestimating it. Because we possess a prayerless state of mind, it is sometimes convenient to believe that this was always the case, that our contemporary deplorable situation need give us no cause for alarm because the past was no better than the present. It must, therefore, be remembered that even if there was much mechanical and much meaningless prayer, there did exist—in Eastern Europe, for example—an atmosphere of piety and a way of life in which communion with the divine was something to be striven for and not to be ashamed of, in which the saint and not the successful businessman, the athlete or the movie-star—the man of the world—was the ideal. Such a pervasive reverence and love for the holy dimension of life could not but touch, to some degree, even the lowliest member of the community and, indeed, at times, succeeded in sweeping great numbers of the people into a pattern of devout worship that transformed their lives.

"Imagine a man," said the Baal Shem, "whose business hounds him through many streets and across the marketplace the livelong day. He almost forgets that there is a Maker of the world. Only when the time for the Afternoon Prayer comes, does he remember: 'I must pray.' And then, from the bottom of his heart, he heaves a sigh of regret that he has spent his day on vain and idle matters, and he runs into a by-street and stands there, and prays. God holds him dear, very dear, and his prayer pierces the firmament."

Prayer was not meant for the saints alone, the unusual among the people; it was meant for every Jew, young and old, rich and poor, wise and simple. Through the centuries prayer entered the very heart of their style of living. Indeed, life itself could hardly have been conceived of without prayer. It is false to think of prayer as a separate division of life, a task to be performed and having significance for the moment but unrelated to the rest of the day. In the life of the Jewish people prayer was part of the warp and woof, a strand of meaning woven into the fabric, the very texture of daily living. Prayer permeated all of life, enriching it, ennobling it, sanctifying it, adding to it in depth and grandeur, providing it with a commentary of divine blessing and guidance.

Until recent times it was common practice each morning upon waking, before they satisfied their bodies with food, for most Jews—no matter what their walk of life—to hasten to the synagogue to nourish their souls with prayer; and each afternoon, at the time of the setting sun, to leave their daily chores, seek out a quiet corner and turn their faces eastward in worship. A frame of reference for the day's decisions; peace and reconciliation at the end of one's labor. Many synagogues had a special *Hevrah Tehillim* (Psalm Fellowship) where after morning worship, simple folk might gather before they went off to work, or in the evening between the services, to recite or listen to an explanation of the Psalms of David. They refrained from making any positive commitments without adding the words, *im yirtzeh haShem,* "God willing." Any piece of good news was quickly followed by the words, *baruch haShem,* "Blessed be the Lord." The first thing a child was taught was not nursery rhymes, such as "three little pigs went to market" or "Humpty

Dumpty," but the prayer to be said upon waking in the morning and the blessings to be made over the food one ate. It was a common sight in the Polish Parliament building to see some of the Jewish members interrupt the proceedings, leave the chamber, and in the hall outside gather together to recite the afternoon prayer. In present day New York one of the officially recognized student organizations at the City College of New York is the Minyan Club.

Of course, there were the three regular periods of prayer—morning, afternoon and evening —the scheduling of which Judah Halevi explained as being parallel to the three mealtimes. For just as the body must be nourished thrice each day, so does the soul need refreshment and sustenance after periods of anxiety and concern. But apart from these three regular services, formal and detailed, we are asked upon waking to render thanks to Thee, everlasting King, who hast mercifully restored [our] soul within [us], and upon lying down, to bless God for the bands of sleep which fall upon our eyes and the slumber which rests upon our eyelids, and to cause us to lie down in peace and rise up again for life.[38] We are told to bless God on every occasion.

The blessing we are bidden to recite over all things that bring us pleasure is man's acknowledgment of God's existence, God's ownership of the world and of His gifts to us. The Talmud

68

juxtaposes two contradictory verses from the Bible: "*The earth is the Lord's,*"[39] and "*The heavens are the heavens of the Lord; the earth He hath given to the children of men.*"[40] Do these passages not contradict one another, since the former asserts that the earth is the Lord's; the latter that it was given to man? No, answers the Talmud. One is true *before* the blessing is recited; the other *after* the blessing is recited. In other words, before a man says a blessing over something—that is, as long as he does not say a blessing—he may think that it belongs to him, completely and totally, that it is his to do with as he desires with no restrictions, no qualifications, no rendering of accounts. In such a case, God says: "It does not belong to you at all. 'The earth is the Lord's.' " But when a man recites the blessing—*Blessed art Thou, O Lord, who hast created . . .* —he acknowledges God as the Owner of all and the Creator of everything, Who but lends to him, a mortal creature, the goods of the world, under certain conditions and with certain qualifications, as a kind of trust for a limited number of years. In such a case, when a man has, through the blessing, demonstrated his indebtedness to God and his acknowledgment of responsibilty for what he possesses, God gives it to him. "*The earth He has given to the children of men.*" This is the mystery of the blessing.

The Jew is obliged to utter a blessing for everything which brings joy (and sadness too), for all the experiences of life. He is told to make not less than one hundred benedictions each day. There are blessings to be said on eating food, on smelling fragrant woods or barks, odorous plants, fragrant spices, on witnessing lightning, on hearing thunder, on seeing falling stars, lofty mountains or great deserts, at the sight of the sea, of strange animals, the rainbow, or trees blossoming for the first time in the year. There are blessings to be recited on seeing a sage distinguished for his knowledge of the Torah or wise men distinguished for other than sacred knowledge, on tasting any fruit for the first time in the season, on entering into possession of a new house or land, on using new clothing for the first time, on hearing good tidings and on hearing evil tidings. The words of blessing travel with the Jew wherever he may go, whatever he may encounter, reminding him that he is not alone in the world, that there is a God who created him, loves him, cares for him—and needs him to redeem the world and restore it to its former harmony.

And how shall one describe the Jewish prayer book? It is a world all of its own, unique in form as well as content. "More than a mere manual of devotion, [the prayer book] is—in a sense—Israel's personal diary, catching, as in a series of exquisite vignettes, the scenes and moments of her entire life, and recording, in a diversity of moods and styles, her deepest and most intimate emotions. Here, for those who have eyes and ears, is Sinai on the one hand, and Belsen on the other; the gleaming courts of the Temple, and the pealing walls of a Polish klaus; the blare of the silver trumpets and the narrow, winding lanes of Safed. Here is Gabirol effortlessly bringing down the immortal to earth, and a Rhineland cantor scribbling his earthiness into immortality. Here is Luria panting desperately after the Celestial Chariot, and Kalir pinning the glories of God to an acrostic."[41]

Because prayer was so intimate an aspect of the people's style of living, the prayer book could rarely be separated from the life of the people. It was a companion along all of life's roads, a loyal friend that never failed to give strength and comfort, guidance and blessing. Apart from the standard prayer books to be found in every home, even poor Jews would save their hard-earned pennies to buy one of the larger editions. What a world of its own were these great prayer books. They were strong, deep treasure chests which one opened with awe and from which one could, time and time again, draw jewels and precious stones of varying sizes and colors, all sparkling and glowing. Such prayer books contained not only the regular services with the prescribed daily, Sabbath and holyday prayers, but also hymns to be sung at the Sabbath table, portions from the Talmud and Zohar for the Sabbath, the Song of Songs (which was understood to be a love song be-

71

tween God and Israel and chanted Friday evening, at the arrival of the Sabbath Bride), a brief code of laws governing the conduct of the services and observance of holidays, the creed of Maimonides, the six remembrance verses, the story of the sacrifice of Isaac, lamentations for the destruction of the Temple and for the exile of the people of Israel and of the Divine Presence to be recited at midnight, the Passover *Haggadah*, instructions on how to erect the booth for the festival of Succot and the prayers to be recited there. Very often, at the end of these prayer books, was printed the complete Book of Psalms, divided into seven parts, one for each day of the week, so that each week, fifty-two weeks in the year, one could recite all the Psalms, until they were as familiar to him as the very clothing he wore. Thus a world of glorious words and phrases fashioned out of the rock of eternity rose to his mind from time to time, as he went about his daily chores and met the joys, sadnesses and tribulations which life holds for every man.

There is a democracy of prayer in Israel. Every Jew wears the *Tallit*. Every Jew who is able and worthy can lead the congregation in worship. It is not a sacrament reserved for a special body of anointed ones and denied to others. Even the last remnants of ancient aristocracy which remain within Israel, the *Kohanim* and *Leviim*, the descendents of the priests and levites, are so emptied of the normal accoutrements of inherited nobility that they, too, strangely enough, often contribute an equalizing influence. It matters not how much wealth or influence a man may have, only a *Kohen* is called up first to the reading of the Torah.

There is an incident that occurs regularly in modern Israel which gives added meaning to this. In the most important synagogue in Jerusalem, in which the dignitaries of the city, including the President of the State of Israel, pray regularly, a strange event takes place. Each morning a slender, middle-aged Yemenite Jew, known as Yechezkel haKohen (the priest), arrives punctually in the synagogue, goes to the closet, removes his work clothes—he is a street cleaner—puts on his only suit, takes part in the morning prayers, and at that point of the service when the priests bless the people (performed daily in Jerusalem), he ascends before the ark, covers his face with the long *Tallit*, stretches out his hands, and he, Yechezkel haKohen, the humble street cleaner from the humble land of Yemen, blesses the great and dignified assemblage. After the service he returns to the closet, removes his only suit, hangs it up carefully, dresses in his work clothes again and leaves the sanctuary to begin his routine task of cleaning the filth from the streets of Jerusalem. For one minute each day he assumes the glories of the priests of old. The wise and

73

the rich bow their heads before him, Yechezkel haKohen, the street cleaner.

How did an ordinary Jew pray in days gone by? Soma Morgenstern, in his moving story *The Son of the Lost Son*, describes the morning prayer of a Jew—not a rabbi, a saint or a great scholar, but an ordinary Jew—who spent some of his time in study—who did not?—but most of his day in hard work to earn his bread and clothe his family:

"He wrapped himself in his yellow black-striped prayer shawl and softly murmured the opening words with ardent lips. His left arm came out of the sleeve of his silk caftan, with the swift movements at which a thousand days of prayer had rendered him adept. He pulled up his shirt sleeve as far as the shoulder, baring the arm for the leather straps of the phylactery which he removed from its velvet bag and kissed. Murmuring the blessing, he wrapped the phylactery around his arm and over his fingers in the prescribed manner. He then placed the second phylactery on his forehead, pulled the prayer shawl over his head and stood there, God's steed, harnessed for prayer.

"Now he sang many songs to the Eternal, old and ancient songs; ancient, old and new melodies. The ancient were sad and mournful and solemn. They are the melodies of those prayers that are as rigorous for the weekday as they are for the Sabbath or for the highest festivals. The old were sprightly, bizarre, joyful.

74

Such are mostly the melodies for those prayers that serve also the Sabbath Day. Nor were the new really new. These are the prayers for every day, the garb for the ordinary working day prayers. They are like the dress of the Jews of this sad Galician land. These clothes hang on restless, humbled undernourished bodies in which there runs old proud blood; they are cut according to the old-fashioned style of a distant land, yet they are so acclimatized to the Slav gloom of this landscape that they could not be imagined apart from it.

"He sang the melodies as his people sing its songs. He did not catch at the songs by their note; he took hold of them by the word. For the melodies are humble and modest like the people; but the words of the prayers, as a part of God, are great and tremendous. Many a melody seemed blinded by the glory of the word. It gropes its way to the light, but without attaining the sense. *And a redeemer shall come to Zion and to them that turn from transgression in Jacob.* The words rejoiced, but the melody lamented, just as much as the melody which sobbed, *O God, look upon our sunken glory among the nations, and the abomination in which we are held as of utter defilement.* Did the melody err? Or the man who prayed? *Exalt in the Lord, O ye righteous; praise is seemly for the upright!* The word exults, the melody sobs. *For we are like ears of corn scattered in the wind, we are like the sheep driven to the slaughter*. On Sabbath days, on festivals, the same prayers may robe themselves in joyous garb of melody; on ordinary days these notes suit them better, notes of affliction and of mourning, of mourning and humiliation.

"Though otherwise calm and gentle, he prayed with the zealousness of those who burn themselves in prayer; as the Hasidim pray. He prayed as he had learned to pray from his father, as a child, as a young lad. The voice of his father who was long dead lived on in the prayers of his son. And whenever the worshipper, now in a solemn mood before his journey, was in danger of straying from the melody or even from the word, the voice of his father came to him and—as a man might rise in the darkness of the room to take hold of a newcomer by the hand as he enters the room—led the voice of his son in the right path. Spirit and body of the worshipper seemed to share equally in the fervor of his prayer.

"He paced up and down the room as though the words and the sentences stood in some secret relation to the number of his paces; as though these were precisely measured to fit the beat of the songs. A word came that was welcomed with a slight bow of the upper body, like a good friend who is allowed to pass with a cursory greeting. Another came before which the worshipper stood still and bowed ceremoniously with bent knees as before an invisible throne. Then came a song which he welcomed by dancing toward it as a jubilant victor. And one came and went from which he parted with mournful, painfully outspread arms, as from the dead. A melody brought a note that expired like the sigh of one dreaming. And another bore a note that broke from his breast like the wild cry of a cossack on the steppe. Once he stood still before the Ark of the Law, drew the hood of the prayer shawl over his face as though to shut himself away in that silence where God dwells, and after that passage was said he flung his arms up in the air and clapped his hands like a child that has suddenly caught sight of a beautiful strange bird in the garden. For the Eighteen Benedictions he stood still against the east wall. He stood there within the magic circle of the three paces, motionless with rigid legs, in blissful devotion, as though a little bird had settled on his left arm where he wore the phylactery. Then his upper body shook violently from left to right, from right to left, and he bowed like a swaying stalk before the wind, swept here and there like a leaf in the storm."[42]

A TREASURY OF JEWISH PRAYER

We have dealt with the meaning of prayer and have seen that it is one of the ways in which God enters the life of man, that it is not an attempt to get something but to be with Someone, a surrendering to the stillness that surrounds us, an opening of our souls to the Source of all souls. It implies another dimension of reality beyond the human to which we try to relate ourselves; it reminds us that man is more than man, that we cannot live without something greater than ourselves. It teaches us what to cherish, gives us strength for life and demands from us that which is most difficult to give—the heart.

We have likewise dealt with the life of the saints and of the common people as it manifested itself in prayer, seeking to discover how the meaning of worship expressed itself in the fabric of human living.

Having discussed both the nature of prayer and those who prayed, it would be well to turn our attention to the prayers themselves. In them we can discover the characteristics of Jewish prayer already mentioned and can therefore better understand why prayer played the role it did in the life of the Jewish people. A Christian scholar, G. Biddle, gives vivid testimony to the glory of Israel's books of prayer. "When we come to view the half-dozen or so great liturgies of the world purely as religious documents and to weigh their value as devotional classics, the incomparable superiority of the Jewish convincingly appears. . . . Certainly the Jew has cause to thank God and the fathers before him for the noblest liturgy the annals of faith can show."

These are some of the words of Jewish prayer:

From the Daily Liturgy

O Lord,
The soul which Thou hast given me is
    pure!
Thou hast created it,
Thou hast formed it,
Thou hast breathed it into me,
Thou preservest it within me;
In time Thou wilt take it from me,
And return it to me in the life to come.
So long as my soul is within me,
I will give thanks to Thee,
O Lord, my God and God of my fathers,
Master of all deeds,
Lord of all souls!

From the Daily Liturgy

With everlasting love
Hast Thou loved the house of Israel,
Teaching us Thy Torah and command-
    ments,
Thy statutes and judgments.
Therefore, O Lord our God,
When we lie down and when we rise up,
We will meditate on Thy teachings
And rejoice in the words of Thy Torah
    and in Thy commandments,
Forever.
For they are our life
And the length of our days.
Day and night will we meditate upon
    them.
O may Thy love never depart from us.

Blessed art Thou, O Lord,
Who lovest Thy people Israel.

From the Daily Liturgy

The Lord shall reign forever and ever.

*O Lord, God of our fathers—Abraham,
    Isaac and Israel—*
*Keep this forever in the inward thoughts
    of the heart of Thy people,*
And direct their heart unto Thee;
*For Thou, being merciful, full of compas-
    sion,*
Forgivest iniquity and destroyest not;
*Yea, many a time Thou turnest anger
    away.*
*For Thou, O Lord, art good, and ready to
    forgive,*
*And aboundest in mercy unto all who call
    upon Thee.*
Thy righteousness is everlasting
And Thy Law is truth.

82

Thou wilt show faithfulness to Jacob,
And mercy to Abraham,
As Thou hast promised our fathers from
    the days of old.
Blessed be the Lord who day by day bear-
    eth our burden:
He is the God of our salvation.

Blessed be our God who hath created us
    for His glory,
And hath separated us from the nations,
And given us the Torah of truth
And planted everlasting life within us.
May He open our hearts unto His Torah,
And place His love and fear within our
    hearts,
That we may do His will
And serve Him with a perfect heart,
That we may not labor in vain
Nor bring forth for confusion.

May it be Thy will,
O Lord our God and God of our fathers,
That we keep Thy statutes in this world,
And be worthy to live

And inherit blessings
In the days of the Messiah
And in the life of the world to come . . .
O Lord my God,
I will give thanks unto Thee forever.

From the Prayers for the Days of Awe

And so, O Lord, our God, let Thine awe
be manifest on all Thy works,
And a reverence for Thee fill all that Thou
hast created,
That all Thy creatures may know Thee,
And all mankind bow down to acknowl-
edge Thee.
May all Thy children unite in fellowship
To do Thy will with a whole heart.
For we know, O Lord, our God,
That the kingdom is Thine,
That power rests with Thee,
That might is in Thy right hand,
And that Thy name is awesome over all
Thou hast created.

And so the righteous shall see it and be
    glad,
The just exult,
The pious break forth in song.
But violence will close her mouth,
And all wickedness vanish like smoke,
When Thou removest the rule of tyranny
    from the earth.
But Thou shalt rule, Thou alone, over all
    Thy works,
On the mountain of Zion, the seat of Thy
    splendor,
And in Jerusalem, Thy holy city,
As it is written in Thy holy words:
The Lord shall reign forever, Thy God, O
    Zion, unto all generations,
Hallelujah.

From the Prayers for the Days of Awe

According to Thy name so is Thy praise:
Thou art slow to anger and ready to for-
    give.
Thou desirest not the death of the sinner,
But that he turn from his evil way and live.
Even until his dying day Thou waitest for
    him,
Perchance he will repent,
And Thou wilt straightway receive him.

Verily, Thou as Creator knowest the na-
    ture of man,
That he is but flesh and blood.
Man's origin is dust;
He obtains his bread by the peril of his
    life;
He is like a fragile potsherd,
As the grass that withers,
As the flower that fades,

As a fleeting shadow,
As a passing cloud,
As the wind that blows,
As the floating dust,
Yea, and as a dream that vanishes.

But Thou art the ever living God and
King.

From the Grace After Meals

Take pity, O Lord, our God, on us,
And on Israel, Thy people,
And on Jerusalem, Thy city,
And on Mount Zion, Thy glory's habita-
tion,
And on the great and holy house
Over which Thy name is called.

Our Father, shepherd us,
Feed us, maintain us,
Sustain us, ease us,
Pray, ease us speedily from all our troubles.

87

Nor let us be in need, O Lord, our God,
Either of gifts at the hands of flesh and
    blood,
Or loans at the hands of those
Whose gift is small, humiliation great.

But at Thy hand
That is full and broad,
Holy and open;
That we be not shamed
For ever and ever.

In Time of Persecution

My God, Thou hast made me hunger,
And, naked, forsaken me
And set me in the darkmost night,
And taught me Thy power and might.

Though Thou burn me in fire
I shall continue to love Thee,
And to find joy in Thee,
As Job said,

"Though He slay me, yet will I trust in
    Him."

Before Going to Sleep

Blessed art Thou, O Lord,
Our God, King of the universe,
Who droppeth the bands of sleep upon
    mine eyes
And slumber upon my eyelids.

May it be Thy will,
O Lord, my God and God of my fathers,
To lay me down in sleep
And to raise me again in peace.

May the Good-Desire control me,
And not the Evil-Desire,
Save me from the Evil-Desire,
And from grave illness.
Let no evil dreams trouble me,
Nor evil fancies.
But let my rest be perfect before Thee.

O lighten my eyes,
Lest I sleep the sleep of death.

Blessed art Thou, O Lord,
Who givest light to the whole world
In Thy glory.

The Private Prayer of Rabbi Hiyya
bar Abba

Let our hearts be united
In the fear of Thy name;
Bring us near
To what Thou lovest:
Keep us far
From what Thou hatest.

The Private Prayer of Rabbi Pedat

May it be Thy will,
O Lord my God and God of my fathers,
That no hatred against any man come
    into our hearts,
And no hatred against us come into the
    heart of any man,
And may none be jealous of us,
And may we not be jealous of anyone;
And may the Torah be our labor all the
    days of our lives,
And may our words be as supplications
    before Thee.

The Private Prayer of Mar,
the Son of Rabina

My God,
Keep my tongue from evil,
And my lips from speaking guile.
To those who curse me, let my soul be
silent;
Let my soul be unto all as dust.
Open my heart to Thy Torah,
Let my soul hasten to do Thy command-
ments.
And deliver me from evil plans, from evil
impulses,
And from evil women,
From all evil that comes swiftly unto the
world . . .
Let the words of my mouth
And the meditation of my heart
Be acceptable in Thy presence,
O Lord, my Rock and my Redeemer.

A Prayer of Rabbi Nahman of Bratslav

Whom have I in heaven but Thee?
And beside Thee,
I wish for nothing on earth.
My flesh yearns and my heart;
The rock of my heart and my portion
Is God forever.

Master of the universe,
Lord of all,
Thou whose dominion is everywhere.
For Thou art the Place of the universe;
Not the universe Thy place.
Give me a heart of truth,
A virtuous heart and pure,
A truly Jewish heart.

May I be worthy
That my heart be the dwelling place of
    Thy glory.

That there be drawn into my heart
The presence of Thy glory,
Great and sacred,
Dwelling in the hearts of each and every
one of Israel,
Thy holy people.

Recited by Jewish Mothers at the Close of the Sabbath

God of Abraham, of Isaac, and of Jacob,
Protect Thy dear people, Israel, with Thy
love
The good and holy Sabbath nears its end;
Now turn to us in tenderness,
And send a happy week,
Abrim with life and health, with bread
and grace.
Let us be pure and righteous, grant Thy
favor,
Untarnished gains and greater strength of
limb.
Amen Selah

I rise at dawn, and there on high
Our dear Lord sits in the seventh sky.
Have pity on me, dear God, and on
My husband and my little ones.

Show me the way, a path that is good;
Thy faithful hand will give me food;
And what Thou givest will be my stay
Today and every day.

The Kingdom of God

It is for us
To praise the Lord of all,
To acclaim the greatness of Him
Who shaped the world in the beginning.
For He hath not made us
Like the pagans of the world,
Nor set us level
With the heathen of the earth.
He has not made our destiny like theirs,
Nor cast our lot with their multitude.

We bend the knee,

Prostrate ourselves
And give thanks
Before the King of kings,
The Holy One, blessed be He,
Who unfurls the sky,
And founds the earth;
His seat of glory
Is in the heavens above,
The house of His might
Is on majestic heights.
He is our God,
There is none else.
He is our King,
There is none beside Him.
As it is written in His Torah:
"Know this day, and lay it to thy heart,
That the Lord, He is God
In heaven above
And upon the earth beneath;
There is none else."

And so we wait for Thee,
Lord our God.
We wait soon to see the splendor of Thy
    might

When Thou removest the idols from the
    earth
And all idolatry is abolished.
Then the world will be perfected under
    the kingdom of the Almighty,
So that all flesh will call upon Thy name,
When Thou wilt turn unto Thyself all the
    wicked of the earth.
May all dwellers in the world see and know
That unto Thee every knee must bend
And every tongue vow loyalty.
Before Thee, O Lord our God,
May they kneel and cast themselves down,
To give honor
To the glory of Thy name.
May they take upon themselves
The yoke of Thy kingdom;
And do Thou rule over them soon
And forevermore.
For the kingdom,
It is Thine.
And to all eternity
Thou wilt govern in glory.
As it is written in Thy Torah:
"The Lord shall reign

97

For ever and ever."
And it has been foretold:
"The Lord shall be King over all the earth;
On that day
The Lord shall be One,
And His name one."

And yet, despite all the poems we write and all the songs we sing, prayer is no cure-all.

It takes us from the noise of the world into the stillness of the soul, not so that we may escape from the world into some mountain retreat or island monastery, but to return us into the world there to perform our task. Before he could know how to lead his people out of Egypt, Moses had to experience the shepherd's solitude in the land of Midian where God found him at the burning bush. The Baal Shem spent the early years of his life in a mountain retreat and far from society. There he strengthened the bonds which joined him to the divine, until he was prepared to disclose his identity and engage in his holy work of redemption. So it is with all of us. Prayer removes us from the market place and the counting-chamber to heal us, to wash us clean, to purify us, to strengthen us, to remind us of what we have forgotten, to let our souls touch the Source of all souls, and then to send us back to the crossroads of life so that we may live out the dreams of prayer. "It is like a beam thrown from a flashlight before us into the darkness. It is in this light that we who grope, stumble and climb, discover where we stand, what surrounds us and the course we should choose. Prayer makes visible the right, and reveals the hampering and the false. In its radiance we behold the worth of our efforts, the range of our hopes, and the meaning of our deeds."[43]

A PARABLE OF PRAYER BY
RABBI ELIMELECH OF LIZENSK

A father and son, who were once traveling together by wagon down a road, came to the edge of a forest where great bunches of delicious berries, sweet to the taste, were to be found. When the boy saw the fruit, he asked his father to stop the wagon and wait for him while he gathered some. His father agreed but told him to hasten, for they could not long delay the journey. The boy, however, delighting in the berries, gathered heap after heap, until the father finally cried out, "My son, we must be on our way, for the moments are fleeting and the road still lies before us." But his cries were to no avail, for the boy's desire was his master. Now the father, seeing that nothing could be done with his son, said to himself, "It would be proper for me to punish him, but how can I, for, though he is foolish, still he is my only child, and the mercies of a father for an only child are manifold." So he at last called to the boy: "Hearken to me, my child, and I shall give you good counsel, so that in your search for the tasty berries you do not lose yourself in the forest, unable to find the path which leads to me.

"When you cry out, 'My father! My father!' I shall answer, 'My son! My son!' Now, so long as you hear my voice, you will know that I hear your voice. But, beware, if you should not hear my voice. Then understand that you are lost in the thickets of the forest, and run to me with all the speed at your command, until you find me."

THE MEANING OF THE PARABLE

This is a parable of prayer. Its simple language harbors profound meaning. It reads like a child's tale, but even the wisest of men can learn from it. From this parable three teachings regarding the nature of prayer emerge: first, prayer is the true measure of every age; second, prayer is the gateway to the Beyond; and, third, life without prayer is in crisis.

PRAYER IS THE TRUE MEASURE
OF EVERY AGE

The parable speaks of a father and his child. It means God and man. For it is you and I whom the Bible calls the "children of the Lord," His first-born son, created out of the dust from the four corners of the earth, robed in the flesh of animals, garbed in the mortality of all creatures who live and die, yet bearing within this robe and this flesh the breath of life

101

He breathed into us. His breath, His life was poured into ours, His image shaped our being, and His divine likeness framed our bodies.

Why were we fashioned in the likeness of the Lord? So that we might strive to permit that likeness to dominate our life, to shape not only a portion of our being, but its entirety, so that we might be like unto Him. As He is just, so should we pursue justice; as He is gracious, so should we be gracious; as He is full of compassion, so should we be full of compassion. Thus, seal and stamp and image and likeness penetrate us through and through until form and content melt into one complete unity.

Created in His likeness, man is the partner of the Lord in the never-ending work of creation. He rides with Him down the great highway of the spirit which runs through the world, as eternity runs through time, and which He would have us follow.

But, alas, though he is God's son, the flesh of man is weak. When he meets the trials and temptations which Satan sets before him, the opportunities for power and pleasure and passion that seem to abound, he leaves his Father and goes to gather a basketful of this pleasure and power and passion. The more pleasure we find—for we are that son, each one of us—the more we want; the more power we obtain, the more we seek; the more passion we know, the more we yearn for. And so, stirred by temptation without and the evil desire within, we wander farther and farther from that great highway and from the side of our Father. He pleads with us to return. We do not heed His call, and so we are drawn on and on into the thickets of the world.

We mortals are foolish children, but each one of us is His only child, and the mercies of a Father for his only child are manifold. How then can He punish us? So our Father in Heaven at last calls to us: "Hearken to me, my child, and I shall give you good counsel so that you do not lose yourself in the thickets of the world. So long as you can pray with fervor and devotion, so long as the hunger for Me has not disappeared from your heart, so long as the love and fear of Me has not gone out of your soul, and in moments of thanksgiving and contrition, at times of rejoicing and sorrow, on occasions of feasts and fasts, Sabbaths and Holydays, even in the quiet of your room or the stillness of the woods, you can still cry out, 'My Father! My Father!' and hear me reply, 'My son! My son!'—then know that all is not lost."

Once we were on that great highway—whose way was straight, where the light shone clear—but now we have forsaken the highway and have strayed into the dark side of the world with its traps and snares, with its false allurements and cheap victories, with its urge to control and dominate, with its never-ending appeal to the aggrandizement of our ego and the swelling of our pride. It is in that dark side of the world, where the divine radiance is shut out, that many of us spend the fleeting days of our years. And sometimes we are so caught up in the mad rush for power, pleasure and passion, which fill our minds and hearts until we care for nothing else, we are so hypnotized by the spectre of our own egos that we can no longer see the great road, nor Him who waits there with eternal patience.

And because we have almost lost Him, we are in danger of losing ourselves.

Yet, despite the weakness of our hearts and the strength of our evil-desire, we are not quite lost in this world of ours, for God, in His eternal mercy, has cast down from His heaven a rope to which, even from the dark, treacherous pit of daily living, we can cling firmly and so still be attached to the Root of the soul. That rope is prayer. It is the bond which joins us to our Father in Heaven, the link which binds Him and us together, regardless of where we go. The house of prayer, in the thousandfold compromise we call living, is an oasis in the desert, a source of new strength to the weary, a place from whch a man can look back from whence he has come and forward to whither he is going and ponder the wisdom of his journey.

Though his days be marked by weakness, folly and sin, the man at prayer finds contrition and the breaking of his proud heart into fragments of humility. He discovers peace and unutterable joy when he hears a call from Beyond. He possesses, if only for a moment, kinship with that from which his soul sprang. He breathes again *the* Breath and recalls once more *the* Likeness in whose image he was fashioned. True prayer with devotion and fervor, with *kavvanah*, is what can save a man, a country, even an entire age. So long as we are able to pour out our hearts with *kavvanah*, we are not lost and our world is not lost. Our souls still grasp that rope which leads back to the Lord of all souls. The ability to pray, then, is the true measure of every age. It means that redemption is still close at hand.

PRAYER IS THE GATEWAY
TO THE BEYOND

According to the parable, the son, in his mad desire for the sweet-tasting berries, is not completely lost in the thickets of the forest. Nor are we lost in the jungles of the world, so long as we are able to engage in true prayer. But a searching question must now be asked. What is true prayer? What is the *criterion* of true prayer and how do we know when a man succeeds or fails at prayer? The answer is as simple and profound as the parable. In true prayer, prayer with devotion and fervor, with love and fear, *one hears something from Beyond.* When we cry out, "My Father! My Father!" we hear Him respond, "My son! My son!"

This does not mean that we must receive a

revelation from heaven as Moses did at Sinai or as the prophets did at a later period in order to have prayed devoutly. It does mean, however, that the essence of prayer is not asking for favors or begging for the fulfillment of our wishes—though this "asking" and "begging" may be important in that they often are responsible for initiating prayer—but the opening of our souls to the stillness that surrounds us, the unlocking of the tightly shut gate over our heart, the rendering perceptive of our spirits to the heavenly voice which cries out to every man in every age in every place, "My son! My son!" This is the deepest meaning of prayer and its ultimate purpose, its innermost content, its soul, its very essence.

THE CRISIS OF LIFE
WITHOUT PRAYER

The warning which the father gives his son at the end of the parable rings frantically in our ears. An alarm has been sounded which only the callous can quiet. Recall the words which the father of the boy at last said to him: "If, when you call out from the forest in which you wander, 'My father! My father!' and do not hear me respond, 'My son! My son!' then understand that you are lost in the thickets of the forest and run to me with all the speed at your command, until you find me."

These are not idle words, at least not to those of us who mourn the loss of prayer in our day, who enter houses of worship but find little worship there, who open prayer books and find no quickening in our hearts, who open our hearts and find—a stone. For we miss the ecstasy of prayer not only in temples made of wood and steel and glass, but also in temples made of flesh and blood. It is so dreary without and it is so dreary within.

How do we know that true prayer is rarely to be found? Because when we pray, we no longer hear that voice which our fathers in other generations heard calling to them from Beyond. We no longer know how to understand the mystery of a moment of silence; we seem to have mislaid the key which would unlock the doors of our heart; we have forgotten how to open the ears of our spirit to that still, small voice which lovingly and compassionately calls to us.

Is it a mistake to assert that sometimes the synagogue itself, because it has been transformed into an institution which more perfectly reflects social conditions than influences them, discourages true prayer and casts sands from the desert into the oasis? Instead of raising the standards of the community toward ancient ideals, the House of God, in a spirit of confusion and weakness, has too often leveled itself to the fads and by-words of the day. In the midst of politics, publicity and the striving for success, as well as innumerable "activities," it becomes difficult to discern the spirit of our fathers in prayers which come easily from the lips but not so easily from the heart. The ancient Temple was built, according to tradition, with its windows wider on the outside than on the inside. Instead of light entering from without to illumine the Temple, it was the inner light of the Temple which illumined the world. This light was the light of prayer which the House of Prayer throughout the ages has cast upon those who dwelt around it. Today the shape of those windows has somehow been altered.

What was once a flame which, in the community of prayer, would spread from man to man, has in our time almost been extinguished by the vulgarity and shallowness of our institutions and our lives. Only a faint spark remains, by some miracle preserved. Our souls have become frozen by the cold world in which we live. We have seen so much suffering that we no longer have compassion for the outcast. Our minds are crammed with so many facts that we no longer have room for awe. We build such magnificent palaces of steel that a sunset no longer fills us with wonder. We have so many possessions that the glory of the stars no longer humbles us. And it must be clear to all who strive for purity and holiness that true prayer can only rise out of wonder and awe and love. Our prayers are mechanical so that, despite new editions, the prayer book remains lifeless in our hands, the dead letters of boredom, the dull humdrum of habit. Rare indeed today is the man who can kindle that solitary spark within each of us by means of the searing flame which consumes his prayer.

It has not always been so.

Rabbi Levi Yitzhak of Berditshev was accustomed to pray with much energy and movement, even though for his own sake less labor would have sufficed. He chose the more difficult way in order to turn the hearts of men to the Lord, for their hearts were broken by means of his example. There was once a skeptic in Berditshev who had come under the influence of the fashionable ideas which had filtered through from the West. The Hasidim, disciples of the rabbi, argued with him and told him that if once he would hear the prayers of their master, he would change his opinions. Scoffing at their words, he went to the House of Study of the holy rabbi the next morning in order to demonstrate to the Hasidim that his prayers would have no effect on him. But when Levi Yitzhak began to utter the words, *A redeemer shall come to Zion, to those of the house of Jacob who repent*, and repeated them a second and a third time with his great fervor and devotion, the smug manner of the cynic was shaken. His wall of new ideas was breached and his heart melted within him. He did not depart until he was brought under the wings of the Divine Presence.

Where do we find in our time of material

riches and spiritual poverty, of magnificent Temples and empty pews, of many prayer books and little prayer, a Levi Yitzhak who, though dwelling in simplicity far from universities and skyscrapers, possessed the golden key of prayer which could unlock the hearts and souls of the most distant and distressed and draw him near to the source of his spirit? Almost two hundred years have passed since the greatest—yet almost unknown—figure of modern Jewry, the Baal Shem, said that prayer is not merely a pathway to the divine, but an aspect of the divine itself, a *portion of the living God*, and that a man must be prepared to give his very life each time he enters the portals of prayer. It is true, the Hasidim rediscovered the secret of worship, but that was across the ocean, in a distant land and long ago; while almost all those who remained in our day are buried in the fertile, anonymous graveyards of Europe. And if, perchance, by some miracle hid from view, a modern Hasid does emerge unexpectedly from our midst, he stands apart as something strange, an anachronism, "in need of proper adjustment."

The message of the parable is clear for us. Our woeful state of prayer stands as a solemn, even a frightening warning that we have become lost in the thickets of a world where flesh has triumphed over spirit. The secret source of strength and renewal which Israel knew in the wooden Tabernacle of the wilderness, in the magnificent Temple of Jerusalem, in the sturdy synagogues of every country and clime, in the modest Houses of Prayer and Study which inhabited each Jewish community, the secret which was known and cherished as a treasure beyond price, despite human weakness within and inhuman persecutions without, the soft mantle of mystery into which they entered each day to draw waters of spirit from the wells of salvation—that secret has slipped through our fattened fingers. The rope of prayer, which was our hope and our promise, has snapped.

With all the speed at our command we must run from the hardness and coarseness of our lives, from the jealousy and anger which rule us, from the harshness and cynicism which threaten to engulf and overcome us, from the pride which blinds us to the needs of others, from the greed which corrodes our spirit, from the enslavement to power and pleasure and passion, from the servitude to the evil desire. We must run until, in a burning fear which can turn into a burning love, we again find Him. For if we seek Him with all our heart and all our soul and all our might, we shall surely find Him Who waits, a loving, yet grieving Father, Who weeps for His lost child and calls out to him again and again, "My son! My son!"

HUMILITY

"The world survives because of humility."

Prayer is the way God enters our life in terms of man's relation to heaven.

Humility is the way He enters our life in terms of man's relation to himself.

THE GREATEST PROBLEM: OURSELVES

The sin of which modern man is most frequently found guilty is that of "self-sufficiency." It is the belief that man is sufficient unto himself and needs no divine authority or guide. It is the certainty that man is capable of fathoming all secrets, of controlling all events, of mastering all situations, even of achieving a utopian society of peace and prosperity which would endure until the end of time. Can we wonder that modern man should feel such a sense of self-sufficiency? To fly like a bird through the air and swim through the sea like a fish; to harness the energy of the sun and uncover the bowels of the earth; to build cities of steel and glass, erect bridges which span the waters and towers that pierce the skies; to unravel the age-old mysteries of nature—all this has led, quite naturally, to the conviction that through his mind and insights, man alone can solve all problems and bring about the millenium. Religion seems superfluous, a superstition, an old wive's tale, and God simply a "father complex."

The experience of the catastrophic events of the past decades, which saw the rise of the Nazi-Communist-totalitarian-man and witnessed a degree of diabolic degradation and depravity unknown before in all human history, should have shattered the modern myth of man's "self-sufficiency." For some it has. Yet there are still those who, dazzled with the material achievements of the past century, are unable to confess the utter failure of man's brief escapade as lord over his universe. There seems to be a devil within that tempts and tries, that teaches us how to strut and swagger, that turns the head and arches the back, that raises the heart in vanity and swells the soul in arrogance. It is to a discussion of this troubler "within" that we now turn.

The discovery of the "self" is modern psychology's claim to fame. The great popularity of this multi-sided "science" is due primarily to the realization that many of man's problems are not brought about by external causes, such as earthquakes, soil erosion or forest fires, but by internal causes of which man himself is the source. The most pressing problem of the age

116

is not how to live with the Asiatics or how to live with the gadgets of science, but how to live with that obstinate, elusive, ever-present self we call the "ego."

It was said of Disraeli that he was a self-made man who worshipped his maker. Power not only corrupts, as Lord Acton wrote, but it leads to pride—the power of a general over his soldiers, of an employer over his employees, of a teacher over his students, and even of a father over his children. An examination of the records of divorce cases in our courts reveals that, while some of them are clearly unavoidable, many are the result of two egos which could not learn to adjust to each other. Even with a beautiful home, children, mink coats, diamonds and a Florida vacation each winter, there is no guarantee of family peace. Likewise if we try to understand the conflicts which arise from time to time among political leaders, economists or even physicists, we always find, to be sure, valid grounds for disagreement, whether it be a question of isolationism, Marxism or nuclear physics. Is it, however, only that? Is there not also embedded somewhere in the complex structure of human conflict, regardless of its level and no matter how objective the issue seems at first glance, the pride of one man struggling against another? There is no escape from the human situation. How to live with ourselves is the problem.

By and large, I think we shall admit, our

society does not hold the humble man in high esteem. Certainly society does not often set him up as an ideal to imitate. Some poets may write about him, some teachers may talk about him, some preachers may preach about him, some politicians may wax eloquent about him, but all of their words do not cause the least ripple in the roaring torrent of the contemporary world. And it is this torrent that bears proudly on its waves the man who is "successful," regardless of *how* he achieved that success, and the man who has "arrived," regardless of *how* he has managed to arrive. The humble shopkeeper, the simple farmer or the common housewife are lauded by "do-gooders" and pandered to by an enormously vigorous army of advertisers; but what really counts in our materialistic society, where we are measured more by what we *have* than by what we *are*, is the man who has property and power in his grasp. He is our hero.

In such a society, humility is looked upon as a formidable obstacle to success, a foolish, outmoded kind of behavior which brings only suffering and the likelihood of being stepped on and pushed around. But the man who has built his house securely, laid away his stocks in the vault, purchased his wife the coat she wanted, bought the car he desired, received the promotion at the office that others yearned for, feels the flow of pride in his veins. He has what others admire, and he knows it full well.

Indeed, such pride is hard to avoid. It often arrives gradually, step by step, almost without our knowledge. Before we are aware, we are in its grasp, victims of one of the most dreaded and fatal of all diseases. "For a gifted man to attain pride is so natural," said the Baal Shem, "that he is scarcely aware of it. It is only when he strives to humble himself in his intercourse with people that he realizes how full of pride he has been. It is like a man who travels in a stagecoach and falls asleep. The driver has to ascend a hill; after he reaches the summit, there is a long stretch of smooth road. When the man awakes and is told he is now on a hill, he can hardly believe it. Only when the descent is made, does he realize how high up he has been."

Rabbi Yaakov Yitzhak of Lublin once confidently expected salvation to come that very year. When the year was over, he said to his disciple the Yehudi: "The rank and file of people either have turned completely to God, or can, at any rate, do so. They present no obstacle. It is the superior people who constitute a hindrance. They cannot attain humility, and, therefore, cannot achieve the turning."

The ego is a wall that, at times, is almost unscalable. It would be well to reflect on the fact that our knowledge, abilities and achievements—all that which raises us above the level of the common man—render us more, not less liable to pride. Simplicity is most rarely found among those who wield the power of ideas or money and have made "something" of themselves in the world. Such persons often think that what they possess in the world, whether it be a beautiful home or a new car, is their *own* creation, fashioned by them and possessed by them for all eternity, something which never was before them nor ever will be after them. Their constant thought is about *my* car or *my* house. That all this is theirs only on loan—*for Mine is the land, saith the Lord*—and will exist in some fashion long after they are gone, and that they are only stewards who hold what they have in trust from the Lord, does not occur to them. Powerful is the pride of possession. It is perhaps less difficult for the poor man to trust in God, for he has little else to have faith in. Not so the rich man. His achievements and possessions cry out to him, "Rely on me, trust in me!" With him trust in God is more difficult.

FALSE HUMILITY

A most distasteful though common trait of humankind is the certainty that one is kind, or good, or pious. How often we hear the words, "I do not believe in God or attend synagogue, but I am a good man." May a good man say that he is a good man? Even worse, however, is the man who says that he *does* believe in God and that he *does* attend the House of Worship, and speaks with the unction of one who is assured that, having fulfilled the outer command, he has received the inner spirit as well. The arrogance of such persons knows no limits and often makes us wonder at the failure of religion to influence them. They seem to go through all the motions of piety, but remain untouched by its splendor. That a man can attend religious services, read from the prayer book, sing hymns, listen to the choir, hear the sermon and then leave without having been changed is a sad, almost incredible fact. Perhaps even *before* he entered, his heart was shut. He was certain that he needed no improvement. Only the man who is critical of himself will listen to criticism from another. Only the man who knows that he is sick can be healed.

The coat of pride has many colors: the plumed purple of outright arrogance, the crested red of overweening conceit, the clear blue of pretentious opinion, the bright orange of garish glitter, the dull mauve of punctilious mummery, the colic green of pernicious jealousy and, most dangerous of all, the deceptive gray of false humility. "The Devil did grin, for his darling sin is pride that apes humility."[1]

Once when Rabbi Pinhas entered the House of Study, he saw that his disciples, who had been talking busily, fell silent at his coming. He asked, "What were you talking about?"

"Rabbi," they said, "we were saying how afraid we are that the Evil-Urge will pursue us."

121

"Don't worry," he replied, "you have not gotten high enough for it to pursue you. For the time being, you are still pursuing it."

The Rabbi of Lublin said: "I love the wicked man who knows he is wicked more than the righteous, for the one is filled with pride which the other does not know. But concerning the wicked who consider themselves righteous, it is said, 'They do not turn even on the threshold of Hell.' For they think they are being sent to Hell to redeem the souls of others."

PRIDE BLINDS THE EYES

Perhaps the greatest consequence of pride, and ultimately its most disastrous effect, is spiritual blindness. When our own ego is the constant center of all our concerns, decisions and actions, and when our own selves are the shining hub in which are set the numberless spokes of life, around which all our thoughts, feelings and encounters revolve in a never-changing whirl of self-centeredness, then we have blinders over our spiritual eyes. We look only upon our own likes, dislikes, prejudices, predilections, desires and whims and not upon those same feelings in other men. A thing becomes important only in so far as it affects our own ego. Our mind turns everything we hear and see inwards toward ourselves. What does it mean to us, for us? We think we see ourselves clearly, but we are blind to those with whom we live and work. We see other men, for they are before us; yet we do not see them, for we are without understanding. This blindness to the interests of others, which is the bitter fruit of pride, is the reason why it is so difficult to maintain any endearing and enduring relation with the proud man. He may be an interesting fellow, talented, well-educated, a clever conversationalist, able to attract attention to himself; but genuine friendship represents more than an occasional story or a "glad hand." Friendship is the gracious meeting of two personalities, the sharing of feelings and attitudes, the ability to understand and even to love one another. This is hardly possible for the arrogant man. He is impatient when someone else talks, and irritable when someone else has the floor. He cannot listen because his blindness bars him from any true understanding of his fellows. And so the proud man, despite his achievements and his cleverness, his abilities and talents, is commonly considered a bore, an impossible fellow, rarely a true member of any group and usually a rather lonely soul. Who can tolerate him? Only those who must tolerate him. A man who cannot see others will not be seen by others. A man who cannot love others will not be loved by others. And is a life without friendship or love worth living?

Pride blinds some of us to the love of our own parents. A common arrogance is that which is found among the children of immigrants who, because they speak without an accent, have attended schools of higher learning and are conversant with a few of the more fashionable ideas, look down upon those who have made this very education possible and who, in many cases, have drawn more common sense wisdom from life's ordinary experiences than their more favored offspring will ever cull from well-bound textbooks. Only after years have passed is that child, now grown up and able to view with proper perspective the true worth of his parents' life-knowledge, able to appreciate the qualities which he had previously ignored. But, alas, such discernment often comes too late. The years of happiness which he might have given to his parents are gone forever.

Let us take a step further. Does the proud man, who is blind to the existence of others and has his eyes trained only toward his own ego, *really* see himself? Blindness toward others may mean blindness toward oneself as well. A man who cannot understand his neighbor may not be able to understand himself either!

The proud man, by the very fact of his pride, is unable to view himself objectively. His own craving to have a good opinion of himself makes it impossible for him to look realistically at his own shortcomings and faults. Having set himself on a pedestal, he cannot afford the kind of examination which might reveal that this beautiful statue is hollow within and possesses feet of clay. When successful the proud man will attribute all criticism which others express of him to their envy, and when unsuccessful he will bear a continual grudge against those who seem to be engaged in a conspiracy to hold him down. Thus the business tycoon who bends his ear to flattery, no less than the constant failure who bears a chip on his shoulder, lives in a dream world in which living contact with himself—not only his fellow beings—no longer exists.

But man can only be truly human if he is in communion with himself, his fellow man and his God. Unless the dialogue within us in which we face ourselves honestly and unflinchingly goes on unimpeded and unless we are open to other human beings, able to love and understand them, we are only partly alive. We fall into the traps of overconfidence, carelessness, inefficiency and complacency that not only injure the standard of our work but affect our very personality. The proud man is blind to his fellow man's existence as he is blind to his real self, because he is blind to God. Having turned from God, he turns from others and from his own true self. Having declared *himself* a god, he destroys the natural harmony into which he was born and rebels against the very meaning of his existence.

AN ENDLESS TASK

The problem of pride is an ancient and a central problem in religion. Nothing is condemned so repeatedly and so emphatically as the sin of pride. "The proud man's sin is as if he had committed every kind of unchastity. It is as if he had denied God. Pride is equivalent to idolatry. Over such a one the Shekhinah laments and God declares, 'He and I cannot dwell in the world together.' "[2]

God cannot dwell in the same world with the proud man, because there is no recognition of Him, no room, no place for Him. We have said that pride blinds the eyes of a man to his fellow man, and even to himself, and that this is so simply because it blinds him likewise to God. No man ultimately worships two gods. If he worships himself, sets himself upon the throne, considers himself an autonomous being who is quite capable of handling all problems that may come his way and the sole cause for whatever fortune may be his, then there is little room in his heart for God. He has no need for God. He is quite self-sufficient. He himself is god.

Everyone that is proud in heart is an abomination to the Lord. My hand upon it! he shall not go unpunished.[3]

Moses understood the curse of pride; he was a humble man, the most humble of men. He knew the nature of his people, knew that, like all other peoples—despite the Torah in their midst—they were human beings, that strange mixture of animal and angel. He knew that they possessed the evil-desire as well as the good-desire and that they could turn away from

126

God as well as toward Him. He was speaking his last words to the children of Israel, for whom he had sacrificed a life of ease in Pharaoh's palace, suffering anguish and rejection. He had led them out of Egypt to Mount Sinai and through the wilderness toward the promised land where he hoped they would turn the great moments of exodus and Sinai and wilderness into a righteous way of living. But he knew also it would not be easy. Thus after sketching their past to them in sharp, clear, never-to-be-forgotten strokes, he uttered a prophecy which was true not only for the ancient Israelites but for all men at all times.

> Beware lest thou forget the Lord thy God in not keeping His commandments, and His ordinances, and His statutes, which I command thee this day; lest, when thou hast eaten and art satisfied, and hast built goodly houses and dwelt therein; and when thy herds and thy flocks multiply, and thy silver and gold is multiplied, and all that thou hast is multiplied; then thy heart be lifted up, and thou forget the Lord thy God who brought thee forth out of the land of Egypt, out of the house of bondage . . . and thou say in thy heart: "My power and the might of my hand hath gotten me this wealth."[4]

Our own hand, held before the eyes, can shut out even the light of the sun.

127

Concerning the verse, *I stood between the Lord and you*,[5] Rabbi Mikhal of Zlotchov said: "The I, the ego, stands between God and us." It is our own self which blocks God out of our life. Our own "I" forms an impenetrable wall, a crust of ego which gradually grows around us, enveloping and blinding us to all except our own interests and desires and, finally, closing off the stream of light which God sheds for our sake.

Rabbi Rafael, who was humble all of his days and avoided being honored, begged his teacher over and over to tell him how he could wholly fend off pride, but he received no answer. Again he pressed his master, "O Rabbi, pride, pride!"

"What do you want?" said Rabbi Pinhas. "This is a piece of work with which a man must wrestle all his years, and which he can never finish. For pride is the garment of God. It is written, 'The Lord is king; he is clothed in pride.'* But God is infinite, and he who is proud, injures the garment of infinity. And so the work of self-conquest is infinite."

"Many a man," taught the Baal Shem, "who believes God is close to him, knows not of Him. But He is close to many a man who yearns for Him from afar. Now you are always to think you are standing on the shore of the Jordan and have not as yet entered the Promised Land. And even though you have performed all man-

* *Ge-'uth*, usually translated "majesty."

ner of commandments, you have done nothing. Therefore, it is written: *These are the words which Moses spoke unto all Israel beyond the Jordan, in the wilderness.*"[6]

The last words of the Baal Shem, he who had searched deeply into the mystery of humility all his life, were the words of the Psalmist, *Let not the foot of pride come upon me.* Indeed, before he died, his disciples asked how they should know who was to be their leader in his stead. He told them to go among those they considered worthy and ask how pride could be cured. Whoever could tell them a permanent way, they would know was *not* the man. "Humility," writes T. S. Eliot, "is the most difficult of all virtues to achieve; nothing dies harder than the desire to think well of oneself." The struggle with pride is a constant struggle, one which we carry on every day of our life and from which no man, rich or poor, learned or ignorant, master or slave, is ever completely free. Do you doubt this? Then try the simple test of not saying that most popular word in the vocabulary—"I"—for just twenty-four hours!

"One must beware of pride," said a rabbi, "for pride needs no foundation on which to build. A man may be lying on his bed, his house may be cold, he may be covered with a torn blanket, and yet he may think in his heart: 'I am great! I am great!'" Pride not only attacks the mighty ones, but those who are lowly as well. It is an epidemic which strikes the poor as well as the rich. "Vanity is so anchored in the hearts of men," wrote Pascal, "that a soldier's servant, a cook, a porter, brags and wishes to have his admirers. Even the philosophers wish for them. Those who write against it want to have the glory of having written well; and those who read it desire the glory of having read it. I who wrote this have perhaps this desire, and, perhaps . . . those who will read it."[7]

GOD'S CREATION

To ward off the hand of pride, which rests so comfortably and so consolingly, so encouragingly and so affectionately upon our sagging shoulders, requires more than human effort. God, in His infinite wisdom, has given us signs which stand as constant reminders that we are creatures in *His* world and not the creator of our world. Each time we bless God for our food, we remind ourselves that *He* brought forth our bread from the earth. Each time we touch the *Mezuzah* on our doorpost, we are bound to think that this house which shelters and protects us is sheltered and protected by *Him*. Each time we put on *Tallit* and *Tefillin*, we are reminded that heart and mind and body are not autonomous units, but are fashioned by Him for *His* service. In the very structure of the universe, too, signs have been set that never pass away, in order to help man remember; creation itself seems to have been ordered for this purpose. When we see the great oceans beneath us, how can we help realizing that we are only drops of water in a world of infinite magnitude? When we see the skies above us, how can we keep from being overcome by their endlessness, their vastness, their wonderful symmetry, against which man is as nothing.

This was the lesson which Job learned from the voice which came out of the whirlwind.

> Where wast thou when I laid the foundations of the earth?
> Who determined the measures thereof, if thou knowest?
> Whereupon were the foundations thereof fastened?
> Or who laid the cornerstone thereof?
> Or who shut up the sea with doors,
> When it broke forth, and issued out of the womb?
> Hast thou commanded the morning since thy days began,
> And caused the day spring to know its place?
> Where is the way to the dwelling of light,
> And as for darkness, where is the place thereof?
> Hast thou entered the treasuries of the snow,
> Or hast thou seen the treasuries of the hail?
> Who hath cleft a channel for the waterflood,
> Or a way for the lightening of the thunder;
> To cause it to rain and land where no man is,
> To satisfy the desolate and waste ground,
> And to cause the bud of the tender herb to spring forth?[8]

And Job replied:

"*I am dust and ashes.*"[9]

Just as man feels his frailty when he stands beneath the vast expanse of the heavens, so does he know his mortality when he contemplates eternity. The wonder of time is as overwhelming as that of space. Creation confronts us with both. Engrossed in filling out the details of the day to day pattern of our lives— sleeping, working and playing—often we fall prey to the illusion that an end will never come, that we shall never grow old, our work never ceasing, our play never halting, that our sleep overtakes us only to freshen us for another waking. Then, suddenly, in the midst of great tragedy or joy, through windows hardly noticed before, we catch a glimpse of eternity and begin to understand that all our life, all our achievement and glory, is as a grain of sand on an endless shore, a single bead in a chain that stretches on and on into infinity.

> *For a thousand years in Thy sight*
> *Are but as yesterday when it is past,*
> *And as a watch in the night. . . .*
> *We bring our years to an end as a tale that*
> *is told.*
> *The days of our years are three score years*
> *and ten;*
> *Or even by reason of strength four score*
> *years;*
> *Yet is their pride but travail and vanity,*
> *For it is speedily gone and we fly away.*[10]

133

Once a busy merchant went to the Rabbi of Lekhowitz and inquired how he might attain humility. While he spoke, the clock struck the hour. He was told by the rabbi that nothing humbles us more than the striking of a clock, for then we know that another hour of our lives has passed, and we should think: What have I done in this hour that has passed and how have I mended my soul during this hour through the service of God?

Creation itself, through space, the overwhelming splendor of the universe, and time, the mystery of eternity, may serve to teach us humility.

GOD'S PRESENCE

But the real answer to pride lies not so much in the awareness of God's *creation*, whether it be time or space, as in the awareness of God's *presence*. Nature is but His handiwork, eternity merely His robe. Sublime as they may be and overpowering as they may sometimes appear, they are not He. They only point to Him, hint at Him, reflect Him. It is the Lord Himself, the realization that there is a living, acting, willing God and the reality of His presence which lays the axe to pride.

The awareness of God's presence brings humility. For, ultimately, there is only one way of dealing with the ego: through the realization that *man is not alone* in the world, that there is a "holy dimension" of all reality which pervades the universe and transcends it; that man is not Creator, but creature; not his own master, but the servant of the Lord. "Not only the Emperor Napoleon declared, 'I am the king,' " remarked a Jewish saint, "but every man who does not enthrone God each day by reciting, 'yiskadal veyiskadash, shmay rabo—Magnified and sanctified be Thy Name,' says to himself, 'I am the king.' " To realize that there is a God in the world is a shattering experience in the life of man, exploding his pride in the tremendous apprehension of the divine, filling him with shame through the discovery of his littleness. The prophet Isaiah tells us how God entered his life when he was in the Temple in Jerusalem. "In the year King Uzziah died, I saw the Lord sitting upon a throne high and lifted up and His train filled the temple. Above Him stood the angels . . . and one called to the other and said:

'Holy, holy, holy is the Lord of hosts:
The whole earth is full of His glory. . . .'
Then said I:
'Woe is me, for I am undone:
Because I am a man of unclean lips
And I dwell in the midst of a people of
    unclean lips;
For mine eyes have seen the king.'[11]

Maimonides testifies how knowing that the King is before us affects the manner of our living.

"We do not sit, move and occupy ourselves when we are alone and at home in the same manner as we do in the presence of a great king; we speak and open our mouth as we please when we are with the people of our own household and our relatives, but not so when we are in a royal assembly. If we, therefore, desire to attain human perfection and truly be men of God, we must awaken from our sleep and bear in mind that the great King who is over us and is always joined to us, is greater than any earthly king, greater than David and Solomon. . . . We perceived God by means of that light which He sends down unto us, wherefore the Psalmist says, *In thy light shall we see light* (Ps. 36.9). So God looks down upon us through that same light, and is always with us beholding and watching us on account of that light. *Can any hide himself in secret places that I shall not see him?* (Jer. 23.23). If we bear this in mind, we shall be filled with the fear of God, humility and piety, with true, not apparent, reverence and respect for God, in such a manner that our conduct, even when alone with our wives or in the bath, will be as modest as it is in public intercourse with other people. Thus it is related of our Sages that even in moments of intimacy with their wives they behaved with great modesty. They also said, 'Who is humble? He whose conduct in the dark night is the same as in the day.' You are aware also how they warned us not to walk proudly, since *the fulness of the whole earth is His glory* (Isa. 6.3). They thought that by these rules it would be firmly established in the hearts of men that we are always before God, and it is in His presence that we go to and fro. Therefore, the great men among our Sages would not uncover their heads, because they believed that God's glory was round them and over them; for the same reason they spoke little. . . . *For God is in heaven and thou upon earth, therefore let thy words be few*" (Eccles. 5.1).[12]

When God enters the life of man, he becomes aware of a higher authority, of interests beyond his own, of ideals that surpass his own self. A sense of awe and reverence settles upon such a man and then his *ani* turns to *ayin*,* his pride becomes humility. His self is attached to a higher self. Neither praise nor scorn have effect now. The ego is no longer the center of his life, but God becomes the center. He understands that the purpose of life is not for the sake of acquiring possessions for himself, nor for the sake of seeking power over others, but that life is for the sake of God, that we are not autonomous rulers of our own kingdoms but servants of the Lord, children of the Most High, created by Him and placed upon earth that we might serve Him through our deeds of love. "How do we know if a man fulfills the verse, *I shall set the Lord before me at all times?*" asked a Jewish

* The Hebrew word for "I," *ani*, consists of the same letters as the word for "nothing," *ayin*.

137

sage. "By his display of humility."[13] In other words, humility is the mark by which the man who dwells in God's presence can be recognized. Humility then is the highest virtue of religion.[14]

> Lord, my heart is not haughty, nor mine
>   eyes lofty;
> Neither do I exercise myself in things too
>   great, or in things too wonderful for
>   me.
> Surely I have stilled and quieted my soul;
> Like a weaned child with his mother,
> My soul is with me like a weaned child.
> O Israel, hope in the Lord
> From this time forth and forever.[15]

IN LOSING WE FIND

We have seen that the pride of man can be turned into humility when he allows the God who loves him and seeks after him to enter his life, and when he becomes aware of a world beyond himself. To know the presence of God is to return His love, and to love God is to serve Him. So it is that the humble man, in turning away from self-concern, turns toward the concerns of others. By becoming aware of a world beyond his own interests and by serving it, he conceives a sense of well-being which is seldom found when directly sought. We tend to find happiness for ourselves when we give it to others. In losing ourselves, we find ourselves.

The humble man is aware of interests beyond his own. By devoting himself to those interests, he solves the problem of his own self. For, strange as it may seem, the more he gives of himself to what is beyond his own ego, the more happiness he himself receives. In one way or another, all of us are servants. The question which we should ask is: do we serve ourselves, our own ego, our own desires and concerns, or

139

do we serve something greater and nobler, something within which we can lose ourselves and at the same time, perhaps, find our true selves?

On an unusually warm spring day a friend and I decided to visit two elderly persons we knew. Each lived alone and each, we felt, would appreciate our visit. We found the first, a dignified-looking man of seventy, seated in a comfortable chair and thumbing through one of the many fine books in his library. He was a refugee who had come from one of the great communities of pre-war Europe. He had been a man of influence and affluence, a man of culture and refinement, who had been held in high esteem. People had looked up to him, consulted him, visited him. His word had been listened to with respect.

What did he talk to us about? He talked about himself. He complained bitterly about his fate, that he was completely unknown in New York, where people did not appreciate him and were unaware of his achievements, abilities, wisdom and knowledge. He complained, furthermore, that those who had known him across the sea now ignored him. Worst of all, he lamented, no one visited him. His home, which had once always been filled with callers, an attractive center for discussion, debate and ordinary talk, was now quite empty. It was, of course, somewhat ironic. While we were paying our respects to him with a visit, he chose to pour out upon us an endless stream of misery and complaint. He was an unhappy old man, a twisted soul who thought of no one but himself. No wonder he rarely received visitors.

From his home we went to that of the second, a sickly widow. She too was an elderly and dignified person. She too was a refugee who had come from the same great European city. Nor was her position in New York what it had formerly been. She was now comparatively unknown and no longer a central figure in the life of a great community. She had come from a distinguished family. She had enjoyed the honor and respect of all and had held high positions in the various women's committees and in numerous social organizations. Many had consulted her and her word too had carried weight.

What did she talk to us about? She told us about kindergartens for children of refugee mothers who were forced to work during the day. These she had founded and still supervised, despite her years and frailty. She told us of the hundreds of scholarships she had collected to send needy and sick refugee children to summer camps. She told us about the orphans for whom she had found homes, about widows for whom she had found husbands, about men for whom she had found jobs, about the poor and the sick for whom she had found help, about those broken in body and soul, in

141

despair, forsaken, to whom she had offered courage and hope and strength. She had talked about others.

She was very happy. She had no complaints. She had learned how to lose herself, to forget the dark tragedies of recent years, the complete change in her life, the destruction of what had been carefully and lovingly built up over centuries. She had learned how to lose all of this in something greater than herself and in serving noble and worthwhile causes that brought healing to those who were ill. A strange, firm calmness, as though some deep, all-pervading force were moving within her, gave this old, frail, sickly widow a semblance of inner strength that brought a sense of peace and faith to anyone who listened to her quiet, cheerful words. To sit with her in her modest living room was to push aside cares and worries, because the very mood and atmosphere of the room would not admit them. Always there was something to be done for others or someone to be helped, and there was no time for complaints or regrets or bitter memories. She was never alone. Her home was always filled with visitors.

So similar were these two old people, and yet so completely different! This was the thought which filled my mind as I walked home that spring afternoon. Both were servants: he served his own ego, his own interests, and found misery; she served the needs of others and found happiness. Is this not both the deepest paradox of life and the simplest truth about living: *the more we lose ourselves, the more we find ourselves?* We never encounter happiness by seeking it directly, by running breathlessly after it; it always eludes us. Only by doing something for others and by forgetting ourselves does happiness come to us, almost mysteriously, of itself. "Him who humbles himself God exalts; him who exalts himself God humbles; from him who searches for greatness, greatness flies; him who flies from greatness greatness searches out."[16]

The more we think of ourselves and concentrate our thoughts on our own concerns, the more miserable we become. The best proof of this is that when we serve only ourselves, we are never quite satisfied. If, like the old refugee, we sit at home and impatiently wait for people to visit us, enough never come; if we constantly seek attention, enough is never given. We are always waiting, always expecting, always searching, always ungrateful. The ego is never completely satisfied.

> *I gave a little tea party this afternoon, at three.*
> *'Twas very small, three guests in all—I, myself and me.*
> *Myself ate all the sandwiches*
> *While I drank all the tea,*
> *'Twas also I who ate the pie and passed the cake to me.*[17]

The world of "I, myself and me" is a small, confining, stuffy, uninviting world. Perhaps the tiniest of all packages is the man who is all wrapped up in himself. Such a man may receive from others the formalities which courtesy demands, but he never receives the outgoing affection of true friendship or the warm intimacy, the sharing of sorrows and joys, of thoughts and experiences, the deep satisfaction which is the handmaiden of true comradeship. For who wishes to befriend such a man, to be close to one who only sees himself and never the people around him, whose sole concern is to satisfy his own needs? He is never aware of the needs of others, nor, for that matter, of his own *real* needs.

A patient in a mental hospital had hallucinations for several years. He thought he was surrounded by an invisible circle whose boundaries he could not cross. Try as he would he could not go beyond the circle. An attending physician noted: "If this man could get beyond that imaginary circle, which is actually a circle of self-interest, he would be cured." After many months of treatment the patient's mind grasped the fact that there were others in the building who needed his help, to whom he could bring a glass of water, a toothbrush, a towel, a newspaper. In this manner, bit by bit, through his denial of service to himself alone and involvement in service to other people, he was cured.

How many people, concerned only with what

goes on within the circle of their own lives, draw this same sort of imaginary circle around themselves and cut off the outside world as if it did not exist. It is a kind of sickness. They may not be hospitalized or put under the treatment of physicians, but they are sick nonetheless. Theirs is a kind of spiritual sickness. Much of the bitterness, the rankling, the inability to get along with others, the misery, the anxiety, the loneliness they suffer originates in this sort of invisible circle that surrounds and imprisons and deadens. Through serving others they not only help to heal them, but they heal themselves as well.

NOT OUR SERVICE BUT SERVING

While it is true that humility leads us to the service of others, and in that service, by losing ourselves in something greater than ourselves, we find personal well-being, a word of caution needs to be spoken. If we are not careful the hand of pride may come upon us even here. We have said that humility implies service; this is one principle. Now we can add a second: the *service itself* is important, not the fact that we serve.

This is what Rabbi Aaron of Karlin once taught:

"If a man constantly examines his deeds to determine whether he is a Hasid [a pious one], it is pride. . . . For what is the essence of melancholy? Melancholy comes about when we

worry: do *I* have, do *I* lack—whether it be of
material or spiritual matters. Everything is important as it benefits *me*. But let us give this
some thought. What difference does it make if
I lack? What is important is: does *heaven* lack?
If our father Abraham wanted to change places
with me, I would not consent. Abraham was
a righteous man, while I am a nobody. Now if
we were to change places, I would become a
righteous man and he a nobody. This would
benefit me, but heaven would not benefit at
all. All this would be only for me, for my sake,
and not at all for the sake of heaven. Therefore,
it is improper to desire it."[18]

The Rabbi of Karlin knew that only melancholy results from too much concern with self.
It is better to forget ourselves in service to
others and in service to God. But—and here is
where he takes us a step further—he likewise
understood that *it is the work which is significant and not the one who does it*. We must
learn to rid ourselves of our blinders, to get out
of the narrow, selfish confines of our own concerns and look at the world from the point of
view of heaven—not what benefits us, but what
benefits heaven—strive to make its point of
view our own. If I were to change places with
Abraham, I would profit in that I would become Abraham. But from the aspect of heaven
it makes no difference at all. There would still
remain only one Abraham and one me.

If we do not stress this second principle,

146

even in working for others our working will
become all-important. We will be acting; but
we will want to be the chief actor. To be sure,
the cause may be a good one, but even the best
cause can, under certain circumstances, become
a source of pride. That we serve others is no
guarantee that the glory of that service will not
go to our heads.

The passage from the evening service, *O
remove Satan from before me and after me*,
means that, "before" we do a good deed, Satan
places all sorts of obstacles and excuses and
difficulties in our way in order to prevent us.
But, what is worse, "after" we overcome his
temptations and succeed in doing our duty, he
whispers: "What a fine fellow you are! You
have taken time from your business, turned
from your daily chores and at personal incon-
venience and financial loss have done this
praiseworthy deed. What an altogether excellent fellow you are!"

The Satan who comes "after" our good deed
with the temptation of pride is sometimes more
dangerous than the one who comes "before."
He often turns our very service to others into
self-flattery.

Indeed, there is a tendency in philanthropic
and religious work to heap honors upon those
whose service is needed. Plaques, testimonials,
gifts, speeches, breakfasts, luncheons and sup-
pers are the order of the day. Every incoming
president must be "installed" and every out-

going one "feted"; every gift must be marked by a name (anonymity is *not* the order of the day); every building, schoolroom, lounge, hall, desk and light must be "dedicated" to someone. Little wonder then that what might have begun as a modest service, inspired by high motives, may end in a struggle for power and a desire to boast. Only if we understand that it is the *service itself*—healing the sick, clothing the naked, feeding the hungry, educating the ignorant, rearing the orphan, caring for the widow—which is significant, and not whether we are first in the ranks of those who serve or last, the chairman of the committee or simply a member, the leader of the group or only a follower, will service to others encourage humility. The task itself comes first; who does the task is secondary. It is important that there be an Abraham; and not that *I* be he.

A king was once engaged in great wars with many countries. To each he sent an army for its conquest. One army was led by his son, the prince; each of the others were led by one of his nobles. When the king's son heard that the nobles were successful in their campaigns, though he himself was not progressing too well, he rejoiced, because the will of his father the king was being carried out and his father would take joy in their victories. But when he heard that the nobles were defeated, even though he was winning his own battle, the prince became sad, because he knew that this would cause much pain to his father the king.

The nobles, however, reacted in the opposite manner. Every noble rejoiced when his own army was victorious, regardless of the progress of the others. And if he heard that the other nobles did not strengthen their position but fell back before the enemy and that he alone was the mighty victor, then he rejoiced even more, for he believed that he alone would be exalted by the king. The will and the happiness of the king meant nothing to him. His only concern was his own happiness and what *he* might receive from the king.[19]

Humility means not serving ourselves, but serving the King.

It also means that our serving is not as important as that the King be served.

IMPLICATIONS OF HUMILITY

Like a deep, broad river which sends forth
fresh brooks that nourish the countryside, so
from humility comes qualities of the soul which
build human character. Service to goals beyond
the self is one such quality. Let us examine
others. How does humility express itself in the
style of a man's life? What does it mean for
the character of a man?

Humility means *gratitude*.

When humbleness teaches us to understand
that we are not the center of the world, around
which all things revolve, but that God is the
center not only of the world but of our own
lives; when we realize that we did not create
all we have, but that we are the recipients of
the accumulated wisdom of numberless generations; that we are stewards of whatever wealth
we possess; that God fashioned the earth from
which our bread comes, formed the rivers from
which our water flows; that the beauty of the
sunset, the affection of our beloved, the miracle
of children, the wonder of kindness, the glory

150

of a smile, the wisdom of age, the vitality of youth—are all gifts from the hand of the Almighty; that this wonderful world, full of mysteries and blessings, full of miracles and joys, has been given to us—then we are filled with gratitude and thanksgiving. "Oh, that men would praise the Lord for his goodness, and for his wonderful works to the children of man!"[20]

Humility means *tolerance*.

Our sensitivity to what others say about us lessens when we admit God into our lives. If the Lord is truly before us, said the Besht, we are able to remain unmoved whether we are flattered or cursed. We do not so easily become angry, do not lose control of our emotions, are not as greatly concerned how words and deeds affect us, for we are grounded in a broader terrain than our own ego and have become part of a course and a way which transcends our narrow interests. In moving our eyes away from our own problems, we see the problems of others and begin to understand the reason for their words and deeds in terms of the conditions of their lives. This breeds tolerance, first, because we ourselves are no longer so all-important, and, secondly, because we are able to comprehend what we did not care to concern ourselves with before.

O Lord . . .
Before those who slander me, let my soul
    be silent.

151

And let it be as the dust, before every
man . . .
For Thine own sake, for Thine own power,
For Thy holiness and Torah.[21]

Humility means *modesty.*

The humble man turns from the honors with
which the world tempts him, because he craves
the honor of God, not his own. He has no
desire to have his name emblazoned on high,
for it is only God's name he seeks to magnify.
He does not elbow his way through the crowd,
eager to be at the head of every line, because
he knows that the other man too must have a
place. He is ready to listen to the words of his
neighbor and is anxious to learn from all men.
Empty of pride, he is able to appreciate the
worth of his fellow and to treat him accord-
ingly. "It is the manner of modesty for a man
to honor one who is greater than himself, to
love one who is like himself, and to have compassion upon one who is lesser than himself."
He lives quietly, within his means, shuns display, dresses simply, is soft in speech, avoids
many words, is polite in manner and calm in
disposition, suppresses his anger and conducts
all his affairs in a peaceful way. This is the style
of his life, because he constantly senses the
presence of the Divine before him.

Humility means *perspective.*

Humility allows us not only to remove the
self-centered blinders with which pride covers

our eyes, causing us to ignore the problems of others and to see only our own problems, but, even more, humility permits us, for the first time, really to see ourselves, without the pretty colored glasses of conceit. From the psychiatrists' offices in recent years has come testimony to the fact that one of the basic problems we human beings face is the problem of understanding ourselves as we are.

It is so easy to escape an unpleasant fact by not facing it and to avoid an ugly truth by ignoring it. Arrogance is an aid to him who refuses to accept himself. It tells him all the things he wants to hear, shields him from all the reality he wants to deny, and creates in him a glowing picture of success, charm and wit where in fact misery and failure have their home. It permits him to live under the illusion that he is quite different from what he really is and that he is in need neither of improvement nor of change.

Living in God's presence, the humble man is constantly aware of a world of values above and beyond him, through whose clear light he is able to peer into the reality of his own being and see himself as he truly is. Such a world of values serves three purposes: first, it provides a standard whereby he can recognize his achievements and his shortcomings; second, it brings judgment upon his present state; and, third, it provides him with an ideal toward which to strive. Thus we see how contrition leads to self-analysis, self-judgment and self-correction. Such perspective means that we are not static, fixed at a single complacent spot of smugness from which we do not and, perhaps, cannot move. We become dissatisfied with what we are and sense the endlessness of always striving to improve, to mend, to raise ourselves. Perhaps the reason why the biblical law of forty lashes was reduced in later times to only thirty-nine was so the sinner should never consider himself completely free from his transgressions but continue to feel that his punishment had not yet been fully meted out and that his ways still needed correcting.

A desire to serve something other than ourselves, the realization that it is the service itself which is important and not the fact that we serve, a sense of gratitude for all we are given, an attitude of tolerance and patient understanding toward the faults of others, a pattern of modesty in our private life and the ability to look at ourselves from a higher vista—all of these help to shape the character of the humble man. Yet, for all our analysis and introspection, it may be that we learn most about humility from the life of the humble man himself. To understand humility it is good to have walked, if only for a moment, at the side of such a man. At some time in our life each of us has known a humble person, though at the moment we might have held him in contempt, because

154

he did not move his elbows with the rest of the crowd. To have had a humble teacher, a humble parent, a humble friend, a humble servant is a blessing we often fail to appreciate until long years have passed and the variety of experience which brings wisdom has opened our heavy eyes to the treasure we once possessed. The humble man, whatever else he may be, is a precious creature, the true nobility of human kind. In his presence we feel a purity of purpose, a sincerity of speech and a clearness of action which invites confidence and trust. Here is one with whom the *Shekhinah* is not ashamed to dwell.

What we seek in others, and therefore in ourselves, is humility. It is not easily found in our confused and harassed world, but it is, nonetheless, worth seeking. "Ever let a man be humble in Torah and good works, humble with his parents, teacher and wife, with his children, with his household, with his kinsfolk near and far, even with the heathen in the street, so that he becomes beloved on high and desired on earth."[22]

THE SAINTS

Through the lives of the Jewish saints the trait of humility runs as a golden thread, joining all their paths and leading back to the Source of all treasures. It is this thread which we detect first and most clearly when we read the stories of their lives, for they wore their greatness in the simple garment of humility, and this cloak protected their wisdom and secured their genius. It was this cloak, too, which drew the people to them in a bond of love that was stronger than life itself, lending both follower and leader the strength which permitted them to survive all catastrophes. In their selflessness they could reach into the heart of their fellowman and were themselves open to the gaze of every true eye. What affection flows from humility, for there is then room for love of others! What great communities were built upon its foundations! What great deeds were wrought along its paths!

Let me recount several tales that will illustrate the role humility has played in the lives of the Jewish saints.

When Rabbi Shmelke and his brother visited the Maggid of Mezritch, they put to him the following question: "Our sages uttered certain words which leave us no peace, because we do not understand them. They are that man should praise and thank God for suffering just as much as for well-being, and receive both

with equal joy. Will you tell us how we are to understand this, Rabbi?"

The Maggid replied: "Go to the far end of the village. There in a small dwelling you will find Sussya smoking his pipe. He will give you the explanation you seek."

They followed the Maggid's directions and came to a broken-down hut which already revealed to the visitor an aspect of the web of anguish and privation in which Rabbi Sussya had been caught from the day he was born.

So they inquired of him: "We asked why it is that the sages advise men to praise and thank God for suffering just as much as for well-being and receive it with the same joy. We were told that you would give us the proper explanation."

Sussya laughed: "I have no idea why you were sent to me. I can be of no help to you at all. You see, I have never experienced suffering!"

Once Sussya turned earthward and said: "Earth, earth, thou art of a better make than I, and yet I am treading thee underfoot. But softly, yet a while, and I will be below thee, thy humble servant."

When the Maggid of Mezritch realized that he had become "known" to the world, he begged God to tell him what sin of his had brought this guilt upon him.

There is a portion of the Sabbath morning prayers which reads:

> By the mouth of the upright Thou shalt
> be praised,
> By the words of the righteous Thou shalt
> be blessed,
> By the tongue of the pious Thou shalt be
> extolled,
> In the midst of the holy ones Thou shalt
> be hallowed,

> And in the assemblies of tens of thousands
> of Thy people, the house of Israel,
> Thy name shall be glorified with song,
> O our King, in every generation.
> For such is the duty of all creatures in Thy
> presence, O Lord our God and God
> of our fathers, to thank, to praise, laud,
> glorify, extol, honour, bless, exalt and
> adore Thee, even beyond all the words
> of song and praise of David the son of
> Jesse, Thy servant and anointed.

When Rabbi Manele, a contemporary of the Rabbi of Kobrin, recited these words one Sabbath morning, he was heard to say:

By the mouth of the upright Thou shalt be blessed—"Manele is not of those."

By the words of the righteous Thou shalt be blessed—"Manele is not one of those either."

By the tongue of the pious Thou shalt be extolled—"Manele is not among them."

In the midst of the holy ones Thou shalt be hallowed—"Nor can Manele be considered among them."

And in the assemblies of the tens of thousands of Thy people, the house of Israel, Thy name shall be glorified with song, O our King, in every generation—"One of these is Manele."

But at the time when the Rabbi of Kobrin was told of this incident, he remarked: "Only a holy man like Manele could include himself among the people of God. But we are too un-

159

worthy even for this. We must continue the prayer to find our place. *For such is the duty of all creatures in Thy presence to thank Thee. . . .* It is only among them that we belong, for, along with the animals, the stars and the flowers, we too are creatures, and so it is also our duty to thank and praise the Lord."

Rabbi Yitzhak of Skvira, a grandson of Rabbi Nahum of Tchernobil, related the following:

"In a small town, not far from Tchernobil, several Hasidim of my grandfather's were seated together at the conclusion of the Sabbath. They were all honest and devout men and at this meal of "the escort of the queen" (the conclusion of the Sabbath), they were casting the accounts of their souls. They were so humble and so full of the fear of God that they thought they had sinned very greatly; and they agreed that there was no hope for them, and that their only redeeming quality was their utter devotion to the great Zaddik, Rabbi Nahum; he, they hoped, would uplift and redeem them. They thereupon decided that they must immediately go to their teacher. They started out right after the meal and together went to Tchernobil. But at the end of that same Sabbath, my grandfather was sitting in his house and casting the accounts of his soul. In his humility and fear of God, it seemed to him that he had sinned very greatly, and that there was no hope for him except in this: that those Hasidim, so earnest in the service of God, were so deeply devoted to him; they would now comfort him. He went to the door and gazed in the direction of his disciples' homes; and when he had stood there a while, he saw them coming."

"At this instant"—so Rabbi Yitzhak ended his story—"two arcs fused into a ring."

A young Rabbi went to visit the Alexanderer Rabbi. The latter expressed surprise and said, "Were I in your place, I would not have used valuable time to visit an insignificant Rabbi like myself."

The visitor replied, "Whom else should the Hasidim recognize as their Rabbi, if not one who holds himself to be undeserving to be one?"

"When a man wants to serve God in the right way and does not succeed," said Rabbi Mendel of Rymanov, "walls rise up before him. His prayer lacks tone, his learning light. His heart rises up against him, and he comes to the Zaddik as one whom his own heart cast out, and stands trembling, waiting for the Zaddik to help him. Then his own humility makes the Zaddik humble as well. For he who is to give help sees the bowed and fervent soul of him who has come for help, and thinks, 'He is better than I!' And at that instant, the Zaddik is lifted to the very heights by his service and has the power to loosen that which is bound. To this we may apply the phrase: 'The ark of the Covenant carried its carriers.' "

A disciple of the Maggid of Mezritch had received instruction from him for several years and was now starting out on his journey home. On the way, he decided to stop in Karlin to visit Rabbi Aaron, who for a time had been his companion in the Maggid's house of study. It was nearly midnight when he reached the city, but his desire to see his friend was so great that he at once went to his house and knocked at the lit window. He heard the dear, familiar voice ask, "Who is it?" Certain that his own voice would be recognized, he answered nothing except the word "I!" But the window remained closed and no other sound came from within, though he knocked again and again. At last he cried out in distress, "Aaron, why don't you open for me?" Then his friend replied, but his voice was so grave and solemn that it sounded almost strange to him, "Who is it that dares to call himself 'I' as befits only God himself!" When the disciple heard this, he said to himself: "I have not learned nearly enough," and without delay he returned to Mezritch.

The Rabbi of Apt was a renowned preacher. But it was this "renown" which troubled him no end, caused him grief and great anxiety, for it tempted him to think well of himself, to consider that, perhaps, it was his own wisdom he was speaking and not that of the Torah. Thus whenever he would be praised on having preached a fine sermon, he would grow angry and turn his face away.

On one such occasion, after having delivered an especially impressive message, a number of Jews began to laud him for his wonderful words. Able to hear no more but controlling his anger, he said to them, "Be silent and listen to what I have to say."

"In a small, out-of-the-way Russian town there once lived a mayor whose life was as ordinary and uneventful as the life of any other mayor of a small out-of-the-way Russian town. Imagine his astonishment one day, when out of the clear blue sky there walked into his humble office the Czar of all the Russias! He was beside himself with excitement. He did not know what to do first. He bowed and scraped and bowed again. He kissed the boots of the Czar, arranged the room and prepared the best chair for him to rest on.

"'No,' said the Czar, 'I don't want all this attention. Everywhere I go people put on a show, abandon their daily tasks, dress in their finery and act their best. For once in my life I want to see my people as they really are, without preparation or affectation. Come, disguise me as a peasant, and we shall visit the town.'

"The mayor, taken aback by the strange request, but, of course, obedient to the Czar's

163

every wish, found a proper disguise and made the Czar over into a peasant. Still unsure, he went to get the Czar's carriage. 'No, it is your carriage we shall ride in.' He offered the Czar his seat. 'No, you sit in your accustomed seat and I shall sit at your feet.' And so they traveled slowly through the village, stopping at every corner and viewing the life of the people. Now wherever they went, the people, seeing the mayor seated in his official place in the official carriage, bowed low, greeting him with the highest respect and honor.

"Imagine how the mayor felt," concluded the Rabbi of Apt, "when he saw the people saluting him, honoring him, praising him—and ignoring the Czar!"

A tale is told of two of the greatest Talmudic scholars of their time, Rabbi Akibah Eger and the Hasam Sopher.

They were traveling by carriage to the great city of Prague. The Jews of Prague were overjoyed at the prospect of the visit and, in their enthusiasm to show honor to the Rabbis, streamed out of the gates to meet the carriage while it was still on the road. The two scholars were immersed in words of Torah, but finally they noticed the extraordinary sight of a great mass of people cheering them and, in their love, unharnessing the horses and themselves pulling the carriage toward the city. Rabbi Akibah Eger, deeply moved, looked out on his side of the carriage at the hundreds of people and wondered why they had come. Of course, he thought, to honor the great sage of the Torah, the Hasam Sopher. I too will honor him. So he got out of the carriage on his side, began to pull with the rest and was quickly swallowed up by the mob. The Hasam Sopher looked out on his side of the carriage and likewise wondered why these people had come. To honor the great prince of the Torah, Rabbi Akibah Eger, he thought. I too will honor him. So he stepped down from the carriage on his side and helped to pull with the others.

When, at last, the carriage reached the city and its doors were opened, it was found to be empty.

Two customs, similar in nature, though deriving from different parts of the world, speak of the power of humility.

When the Emperor of Austria-Hungary was to be crowned, it was traditional to bring him to the gates of the Saint Stephen Cathedral in Vienna. There he was asked by the priests:

"Who wishes to enter?"

"The Emperor Franz Joseph of Austria-Hungary wishes to enter."

"We do not know the Emperor Franz Joseph of Austria-Hungary. Who wishes to enter?"

"Franz Joseph wishes to enter."

"We do not know Franz Joseph. Who wishes to enter?"

"A sinner wishes to enter."

"We know a sinner. Enter."

In India a like custom prevailed. When a new prince was to be appointed, he was taken to a certain temple which contained seven great rooms that led to the innermost chamber where the shrine of Buddha rested. At the doorway to each room the prince had to pause and utter the words, "Am I a human being?" With each recital, the glory of his new office receded further into the background until, by the time he reached the innermost room, he had fallen low enough to be raised to princedom.

Perhaps the second custom is more acceptable to the Jewish spirit than the first, which emphasizes over-much the element of sin. We are reminded how among the people of Israel until recent times, it was not uncommon for a rabbi, who feared that his learning and fame and the words of admiration he constantly heard were stirring up feelings of pride, to leave the city of his renown, don the clothes of a beggar and, leaving his money and possessions at home, wander, unknown, from village to village, begging for his living, until the hardships he endured and the curses flung at him served to destroy his pride and break his heart, until he had become humble once again.

TOO MUCH HUMILITY

Let us pause for a moment and make a qualification:

There is danger in too much humility.

Some modern psychologists have criticized the religious doctrine of humility, which they depict as one of the most dangerous consequences of what they call the "authoritarian conscience." "[The religious] man," writes Erich Fromm, "curbs his own powers by feelings of guilt, rooted in the authoritarian conviction that the exercise of his own will and creative power is a rebellion against the authoritarian prerogatives to be the sole creator and that the subject's duty is to be his 'things.' . . . To be aware of one's powerlessness, to despise oneself, to be burdened by the feeling of one's own sinfulness and wickedness are [for the religious man] the signs of goodness. . . . The very fact of having a guilty conscience is in itself a sign of one's virtue, because the guilty conscience is the symptom of one's 'fear and trembling' before the authority. . . . Most religious . . . systems in the history of mankind could serve as illustrations of the authoritarian conscience."[23]

Fromm criticizes the traditional conception of humility because it seems to crush man's dignity and to trample underfoot the worth of his personality. He sees it as part of an authoritarian pattern in which the self must be humiliated before the divine tyrant in order to be accepted. Against this view he maintains that the true love of others presupposes self-love. *Thou shalt love thy neighbour as thyself.* In order to have that respect for the human personality which expresses itself in the love of our neighbor, we must love ourselves, because we too are human.

The difference between Fromm's views and those of Judaism are more verbal than real. Judaism never denied the unique worth of each soul. "Only one single man was created in the world," wrote the sages, "to teach that, if any man has caused a single soul to perish, Scripture imputes it to him as though he had destroyed a whole world; and if any man saves a single soul, Scripture imputes it to him as though he had saved a whole world. . . . Again, but a single man was created to proclaim the greatness of God, for man stamps many coins with one die, and they are all like to one another; but God has stamped every man with the die of the first man, yet not one of them is like his fellow."[24] "When a man goes on his road, a troop of angels proceed in front of him and proclaim, 'Make way for the image of the Holy One, blessed be he.' "[25]

Because Judaism places such high worth in man, seeing in him God's image on earth, it is aware of the danger in puffing up the ego. Judaism does not tell us to deny the self, but rather to integrate it. The call to humility does not mean that we should suppress our human worth, but that we should realize we are man, not God.

Strangely enough, it is the philosopher Maimonides who, praising the golden mean in all other virtues, sets it aside when discussing humility and asserts that the practice of this virtue has no limit; while the man of mysteries, the Baal Shem, who founded a movement which emphasizes humility, issues a warning. He tells us that man, through overmuch humility, may fall into the trap of despair, thinking himself utterly worthless, filled with sin and wracked by passion. For then he forgets that to him alone is given the power to create and build, to think and pray; that he is God's partner in the daily work of creation, but little lower than the angels, crowned with glory and honor, having dominion over the works of God's hands; that, above all creatures, he is important in the universe; that he alone can hear God's word and bring about His Kingdom, for as the Zohar says, "What is wrought in heaven is wrought first on earth." Such forgetfulness, the Baal Shem adds, is the very work

169

of Satan. Humility which leads to a feeling of helplessness and despondency, which crushes the spirit through the belief in man's own impotency, his utter worthlessness, which destroys God's image in man so that he forgets he is the King's son, is fraught with the darkest of dangers and must be earnestly opposed.

Rabbi Simhah Bunam once told his pupils that everyone should have two pockets, so that, according to his needs, he can reach into the one or the other. In his right pocket is to be a slip of paper with the words, *For my sake was the world created,*[26] and in his left pocket one with the words, *I am dust and ashes.*[27] There is a time for each.

Humility is not a kind of weakness, as some are prone to believe, as a result of which one is stepped on and pushed around. It is not the lack, but the presence of something; not weakness, but a strength in that which is higher than the self. The life of Moses provides clear evidence. He was the greatest of all the prophets, the man to whom God spoke face to face, the fearless antagonist of the mighty Pharoah, the strong leader of a rebellious people, the ideal of all mankind. How does the Bible describe him? *Now the man Moses was very humble, above all the men that were upon the face of the earth.*[28] Who can measure the greatness of Moses? The Jews had sinned; they had made and worshipped the golden calf. God threatened to destroy them and to make Moses the father of a new people. You will be the founder of a new nation, God told him. I shall no longer be the God of Abraham, Isaac and Jacob. I shall be the God of Moses! It was the greatest temptation a man has ever faced. But Moses replied, *Forgive the people; and if not, blot me out of Thy book*.[29] He was only a servant, a vessel. Of what importance was his life apart from the people? Here for all ages is the supreme symbol of the humble man. Is it the symbol of a weakling, or of one who was lacking in self-confidence? Certainly not. The total selflessness of Moses was not the selflessness of timidity, but the selflessness of dedication to God. And it was such power of dedication, singlemindedness of purpose, completeness of action, that carried the people to the high levels of faith in God. The humility of Moses stemmed from his being a servant of both the Lord and the people, and it was this very service which bestowed invincible strength upon him.

The humble man is attached to something greater than himself. He understands that man is more than man, and that the life of man is part of the life of God. This sense of attachment to what is greater than himself, of being the channel which carries water from an endless reservoir, gives him strength. He knows that what he does is not for self-glory, but for the glory of that which is beyond himself.

171

Knowing this, he is not afraid to face the world. On the contrary, he considers it his duty.

Humility does not mean that we must go about with bent head, shuffling gait and unkempt clothes, speaking to no one, hiding from society, afraid of other men. The Lord requires not a broken body, but a broken spirit. It does not mean a denial of the world or of our talents. The world is the stage and we are the players. Humility does not remove us from the cast; it simply gives us a new role and teaches us something we did not know before of the nature of the play. We must use our talents, our abilities, our genius, and not suppress them; we must accept the task assigned to us, and not withdraw from it. The fear of fame and the pride it may bring does not mean that man must avoid all honor, all success, all achievement, which are rightfully his, and, separating himself from society, deny the world the benefit of his talents. He must use his talents, display his abilities, achieve what he was meant to achieve; but always he must keep in mind that ultimately this success and this accomplishment are not his. They have been given to him for a purpose; he is the messenger of someone greater than himself for whose sake he lives and acts and uses his talents.

A king once wanted to learn the secret of humility. To achieve it, he wore sackcloth on his body, put ashes on his head, denied himself food and water, left his royal palace to live in a hovel in poverty, employed men to curse and beat him, and afflicted himself with every kind of misery. It was to no avail. He felt more proud now than ever before.

A wise man then showed him the way: "Dress like a king, live like a king, act like a king; but let your heart be humble."

GOD LOVES THE HUMBLE

It is the humble man whom God loves best, for he is closest to Him. He reaches down to all men, seeking to touch them and embrace them and be near to them; but He is repelled by the door of pride, as it is written regarding the arrogant man, "I and he cannot dwell in the same world." The humble man has no door, only an open threshold into his days and months and years, only an invitation to the Lord of all worlds to enter his life. Herein lies the divine paradox of transcendence and immanence: He who is above all the heavens, beyond all the thoughts of men and praises of angels—Creator, Revealer, Redeemer—is at the same time near to the lowliest of men, close to their hearts—Hope, Refuge, Salvation.[30]

> *Thus saith the Lord:*
> *"The heaven is My throne,*
> *And the earth is My footstool;*
> *Where is the house that ye may build unto*
> *Me?*
> *And where is the place that may be My*
> *resting place?*

174

For all these things hath My hand made,
And so all these things came to be,
Saith the Lord;
But on this man will I look,
Even on him that is humble and of a con-
trite spirit,
And trembleth at My word."[31]

For thus saith the High and Lofty One
That inhabiteth eternity, whose name is
holy:
"I dwell in the high and holy place,
With him also that is of a contrite and
humble spirit,
To revive the spirit of the humble,
And to revive the heart of the contrite."[32]

The Bible cries out for humble men. They
are the dearest friends of the Lord. "Of all the
sons of man, none are so near to the Supreme
King as those vessels, a broken heart and a
contrite spirit, which he uses, as it is written,
*The Lord is nigh unto them that are of a
broken heart, and saveth such as are of a contrite spirit.*"[33] God is drawn to the humble
and the self-critical, although society may cast
them out; He is driven away from the arrogant
and the self-assured, even though society may
clasp them to its bosom. He loves the humble,
lowly souls who feel His presence in their lives
and, like children of a loving father, walk mod-
estly by His side.

The Psalmist wrote, *If I ascend up into*

175

*heaven, Thou art there; if I make my bed in
the nether world, here Thou art.*[34] Rabbi Uri
of Strelisk explained this as meaning: "When
I consider myself great and think I can touch
the sky, I discover that God is far away there;
and the higher I reach, the farther away He is.
But if I make my bed in the depths, if I bow
my soul down to the nether world, He is here
with me."

"All the prayers, all the mitzvot and all the
Torah of Israel aim only to draw the Shekhinah
down to dwell in our midst. And its dwelling
place is a broken and contrite heart."

To be a Jew means to exercise humility.
According to the Talmud, if a man is full of
arrogance, it is a sign that his ancestors did not
stand at Sinai to receive the Torah. "The words
of the Torah are likened to water, as it is written, *Ho, everyone that thirsteth, come ye to
the waters,*[35] to indicate that just as water leaves
high places and goes to low places, so the words
of the Torah leave the haughty and stay with
the humble."[36] Indeed, Sinai itself was chosen
over all the other higher mountains to be the
place of revelation as a sign that the word of God
seeks the lowly and humble. Nor was Israel
selected from the other nations for her power
or size. *Thou art a holy people unto the Lord
thy God: The Lord thy God hath chosen thee
to be His own treasure, out of all peoples that
are upon the face of the earth. The Lord did
not set His love upon you, nor choose you, be-*

176

cause ye were more in number than any people
—for ye are the fewest of all peoples.[37] And this
people, the fewest of all the peoples, a people
taken out of slavery, redeemed from bondage—
a slave people—was called to the humble Mount
of Revelation to hear the word of God which
only the humble could hear for only the humble would listen. They heard and they obeyed
and remained humble. "God said to Israel, 'I
love you, because even when I shower greatness
upon you, you make yourself small before
Me.' "[38]

If standing in His presence brings humility,
then Israel should be the most humble of
peoples, for they "stood at Sinai" before the
ineffable glory and splendor of His majesty,
when for all time He revealed His will to mankind. The experience of this standing in His
presence is graven indelibly with a pen of fire
and thunder and lightning in the memory of
our people, recalled each day of our lives,
harked back to at every opportunity. Thus the
festival of Shavuot is referred to as the "Time
of the *giving*" (not "when He *gave*") "of our
Torah"; and when a Jew is called to the reading
of the Law, he recites, *Blessed art Thou, O
Lord our God King of the universe who gives*
(not "*gave*") *us the Torah*. God is *constantly*
giving Israel the Torah. Not only did the generation which went forth from Egypt stand at
Sinai; all the generations stood there. We are
taught to stand at Sinai again and again. It is

177

a never-ending experience. Above all peoples, the people of Israel moves and lives and carries out its existence in His presence, for He has set His name over us, put His words in our mouth and covered us with the shadow of His hand. So long as we are conscious of His presence, in the past as well as in the present, so long as we do not forget the image in which we were created, Him of whose life we are a part, where we have come from, whither we are going and the holy task which has been entrusted to us—Israel must remain humble.

To forget is tempting. No longer to remember that we are the king's son and become like all the nations, putting our faith in the work of our own hands, is a constant threat. Perhaps one of the reasons we have been driven from land to land, suffering privation and persecution, denied the security of power and wealth and country, is to remind us—lest we so easily forget—that, ultimately, there is no humanly fashioned security, that pride of possession is vanity. Thus the course of history itself has sought to breed humility in our very bones.

Let us not think that when humility has once been acquired, it is thereafter an inheritance. It is a virtue which must be constantly struggled for, won only to be lost again a thousand times, the most elusive of qualities, but, nonetheless, among the most valuable. Man is the least static of creatures. What he is born into is no guarantee of what he will become.

When Alexander the Great had returned from his many victories over the nations, according to legend, he called all of his army together and declared, "Now that we have conquered the greatest and most powerful peoples of the earth, let us prepare to do battle with yet a greater foe—ourselves." Each of us possesses an ego and each of us is engaged in an endless struggle, not only with the world about us, for the survival of our bodies, but with the world within us, for the survival of our souls. It is only by throwing open the heavy doors of the spirit and letting God enter our lives through the wonder of humility that we learn how to fight that battle and how to live with ourselves.

COMPASSION

Blessed be He who hath compassion upon the earth;
Blessed be He who hath compassion upon His creatures."

Prayer is the way God enters our life in terms of man's relation to heaven.

Humility is the way God enters our life in terms of man's relation to himself.

Compassion is the way God enters our life in terms of man's relation to his fellowman.

HARDNESS OF HEART

Just as prayer and humility are rare in our time, so is compassion rare in our world today. Indeed, there are some who, far from lamenting its absence, see this as something desirable, something to be striven for. To them compassion is not a benefit but a detriment, not a boon but a sign of weakness. Their teachings on this subject symbolize much of the attitude of the modern age. "Pity," writes Nietzsche, "is opposed to the tonic passions which enhance the energy of the feeling of life; its action is depression. A man loses power when he pities. On the whole, pity thwarts the law of development which is the law of selection. It preserves

183

that which is ripe for death. It fights in favor of the disinherited and the condemned for life; thanks to a multitude of abortions of all kinds which it maintains in life, it lends life itself a sombre and questionable aspect. Nothing is more unhealthy in the midst of an unhealthy modernity than . . . pity."[1] Earlier in the same work, Nietzsche sheds tears of grief over the beautiful "blond beasts" (his phrase) of Germany whom religion had caged in and perverted by the subversive doctrine of compassion.

Nietzsche has had his way. Compassion was removed from that Teutonic beast and the world has been able to view it in all its ghastly, "pristine" beauty. Nazism arose, when this philosopher and others like him were taken seriously, when the mask of pity was removed from the monster which hid beneath. We have witnessed and still are witnessing one of the horrors of the ages: whole nations devoted to cruelty, to hatred, to passion. We have seen in its naked fury the wickedness which lies loosely chained in the dark depths of the human breast, for there has arisen a new man, a totalitarian man, who has cast off the cloak of Western Civilization, the garb of Christianity and reverted to his beast-like ancestors whose power was the fist of might and whose food was a feast of blood.

Heinrich Heine, the assimilated German-Jewish poet, was one of the few whose troubled eye pierced the veil of the future. He wrote:

184

"Christianity—and this is its noblest merit—mitigated in a measure that brutal Germanic lust for war; it could not destroy it, however. Should the taming talisman, the cross, shatter some day, there will then burst forth again the ferocity of the old warriors, the insane frenzy of which the Nordic poets sing and speak so much. The talisman is decaying and the day will come when it will woefully break down. The old stone gods will then rise from the long-forgotten ruins, rub the thousand-year-old dust from their eyes, and Thor with his giant sledge-hammer will, in the end, leap forth and smash the Gothic cathedrals."[2]

Even Heine, however, was unable to foresee that the breeding ground of the new man-beast would not be limited to Germany alone, but would spring up as an uncontained epidemic of destruction in many countries. The defeat of the Nazis has meant neither the defeat of Nazism and Fascism nor a quieting of the spirit of inhumanity with which they were imbued. It has not meant the elimination of the man-beast, spawned in the muck of the corrupted soul, which is the legacy of our time. This hydra-headed monster replaces one lost limb with ten new ones. Instead of one Hitler we now have ten tyrants—none, perhaps, so demonic at the moment, but all potentially his like. The present Communist menace is as fearful as the past Nazi menace. The spectre of the new man-beast has risen out of the dregs

185

of humanity in more lands than we should care to admit and seeks to embrace the entire world in its satanic grip of hate and death.

Compassion shuns our world. There has been so much cruelty and suffering that the senses have become dulled; so much spilled blood that its sight no longer frightens us; so many rotted bodies that their stench no longer sickens us. Where were the democratic nations, our allies and friends, where was our own land of liberty and freedom, when human beings were being slaughtered in the charnel houses of Europe? Where were many of us? Do not think that we have remained unaffected. The festering hand of moral leprosy has touched us as well. Our feelings, too, have been ravished by the disease. The cruelty of our times, so enormous and so continuous, has had its effect on everyone of us.

In May of 1943, the Jews of the Warsaw Ghetto, enslaved, starved, burned alive, only a fragment of their original number remaining, decided to revolt against the Nazis. If they had to die, they might at least die fighting. This was the last moment, the final convulsion, in the destruction of Polish Jewry which had begun late in 1939, when Poland capitulated to the onrushing hordes. At this late date messages were still somehow being smuggled out to the world at large. Theirs was a frantic hope that something would yet be done to save them. It is commonly agreed today that many of these noble martyrs could have been rescued if immediate and decisive action had been taken.

Among the Polish Government in Exile in London were several Jewish leaders. They were the sole, slender link between those caught in the death trap and the outside world. One of these, Shmuel Zygelboim, who had been a representative to the Nazis from the Jews in the Warsaw Ghetto, miraculously escaped, fled to London to plead for his people and finally committed suicide, stating his reasons in a letter, the searing words of which should be engraved upon the eternal conscience of the world.

The final letter of farewell addressed by Zygelboim to the Polish President and Prime Minister.

I am taking the liberty of addressing my last words to you, and through you to the Polish government, to the Polish people, to the governments and peoples of all allied nations, and to the conscience of the world.

The last news received from Poland makes it clear that the Germans are determined to wipe out, with horrible brutality, the last remnants of the Jews who have survived in Poland. Behind the walls of the ghetto is now going on the last act of a tragedy unequalled in all history. The murderers themselves bear the primary responsibility for the crime of extinction of the whole Jewish population of Poland, but, indirectly, this responsibility also weighs on all humanity, on the peoples and governments of the allied nations, because they have not made any attempt to do something drastic to stall the criminal deeds. By looking on indifferently while helpless millions of tortured children, women and men were murdered, those nations have associated themselves with the criminals.

I wish to declare that the Polish government, although it has sought to influence the public opinion of the world, has not done so sufficiently. It has not taken any steps commensurate with the enormity of the drama that is now happening in Poland. Out of nearly three and a half million Polish Jews and seven hundred thousand Jews deported to Poland from other countries, there have survived, in April of 1943—according to a report of the leader of the Underground—only three hundred thousand! And the extermination continues.

I cannot be silent. I cannot live while the remnants of the Jewish population of Poland, of whom I am a representative, are perishing. My friends in the Warsaw Ghetto died with weapons in their hands in a last heroic battle. It was not my destiny to die together with them, but I belong to them in their mass graves.

By my death I wish to make my final protest against the passivity with which the world is looking on, permitting the extermination of the Jewish people.

I know how little human life is worth today, but as I was unable to do anything during my life, perhaps by my death I shall contribute to breaking down the indifference of those who may now at the last moment rescue the few Jews still alive.

My life belongs to the Jewish people of Poland and therefore I give it to them.

I am sure that the President and the Prime Minister will convey my words to those to whom they are addressed and that the Polish government will soon begin all possible diplomatic action on behalf of those Polish Jews who are still alive. I bid farewell to all that was dear to me and that I have loved.

Shmuel Zygelboim[3]

Unbelievable though it may sound, the truth is that Zygelboim's tragic death, like his life, was for naught. His words, if read at all, may have caused a momentary pause in the minds of some of the more sensitive, but they were ignored by those whose influence counted most and who could have helped, elected representatives and appointed diplomats, masses and leaders, Gentiles and Jews.

The only answer was the cold, official, polite inhuman language of silence.

The absence of compassion in our time can be seen, however, not only in the unbelievable enormities which the twentieth century tolerates, the record of which even the most hardheaded historians of future generations will ponder over, wonder at and only slowly come to believe. The absence of compassion can likewise be discerned in the commonplace activities of our daily life which, though never to be recorded in history books, are in some ways equally important for an understanding of the toughness of our world and of our own personal lives. We cannot be concerned with the lack of compassion on a historic scale without also being made aware of a lack of compassion in the individual lives of those about us, our friends and acquaintances, and, more important, with a lack of compassion in our very own lives.

Do we resist the temptation to insult, or do we spit forth arrows of fire at the nearest target? Do we forgive a wrong, or do we harbor for long years the acid feelings of revenge? Do we remember that our competitor, too, must earn his daily bread, or do we crush him in our mad rush for power? Do we feel the pain of one who lies ill, or do we look on with cold, fitful eyes? Do we treat rich and poor alike, or do we grovel before the one and sneer at the other? Do we know something of the pain of our friend when he pours out his woes to us, or do we listen with a cold heart? Do we offer a helping hand to the needy relative, or do we go out of our way to avoid meeting him? Do we assist the blind to cross the street, or do we hurry on, confident that someone else will do it? Would we bend down toward the mire to pull an unfortunate man from it, or would we be too concerned about soiling our clothes?

All this must sound insignificant, even banal, and bring a smile to the reader's lips. Perhaps it is insignificant when compared to the death of millions in extermination camps; but these seeming trifles, unchecked and untended, can grow into mass-murder. Let us never forget that compassion concerns not only great issues but small ones as well. In both, the world and we have grown callous, dangerously callous.

The heart of man, the Bible tells us, is deceitful above all else. There, hidden in the depths—away from his false smile, his easy handshake, his cordial conversation, his expressions of affection, even his deeds of friendship—the terrible fires of hate burn fiercely. That is why the verse, *Thou shalt not hate thy brother in thy heart*,[4] cannot mean that a man might think, "I must not strike him, nor beat him, nor curse him, but I may hate him." It says, *in thy heart*.[5] Truly, *The heart is deceitful above all things. It is exceedingly weak. Who can know it?*[6]

A long confession of sins is recited several times during the solemn service of the Day of Atonement. There is the sin of slander, of wronging one's neighbor, of offending parents and teachers, of lying, of cheating, and many more. But there is one sin in the confession which stands out from all the others—the sin of a hard heart—because it is involved in all of the others. The sins of men are without number; they are with us each day in different forms, intensities and effects. They may have various causes, depending on the particular sin and the particular situation; but one cause that flows into the roots of almost every transgression is the hard heart. It is to be found somewhere at the bottom of almost all human wickedness and deceit, the touchstone of almost all human misery. This is the reason why, when the list of one's sins is recited on the Day of Atonement, the day of confession and contrition, we strike our heart at the mention of each sin. And we pray that the words of the prophet may come to pass:

> *A new heart will I give you*
> *And a new spirit will I put within you;*
> *And I will take away the stony heart out of*
>   *your flesh,*
> *And I will give you a heart of flesh.*[7]

God says:

> For a small moment have I forsaken thee; but with great mercies will I gather thee. In a little wrath I hid my face for a moment, but with everlasting kindness will I have compassion on thee.
>
> For the mountains shall depart, and the hills be removed; but my kindness shall not depart from thee, neither shall my covenant of peace be removed, saith the Lord that hath mercy on thee.[8]

And Israel responds:

> O Thou who art all-good, whose mercies never fail us, Compassionate One, whose loving-kindnesses never cease, we ever hope in Thee.
>
> Blessed be He who hath compassion upon the earth. Blessed be He who hath compassion upon His creatures.[9]

The compassion of God points the "way" for man, for when a man acts compassionately, he is walking in the "way" of the Lord. This is the meaning of *imitatio Dei*.

Rabbi Hama ben Hanina said:

"It is written: *After the Lord your God shall ye walk.*[10] How are we to understand this? Is it possible for a man to walk after the presence of God? Is it not written, *For the Lord thy God is a devouring fire?*[11] What it means is that we shall walk after the attributes of the Holy One, blessed be He.

193

"As He clothes the naked—for it is written, *And the Lord God made for Adam and for his wife garments of skins, and clothed them*[12]— thus you also shall do: you shall clothe the naked.

"The Holy One, blessed be He, visited the sick, as it is written, *And the Lord appeared unto Him by the terenbinths of Mamre.*[13] Thus you shall also do: you shall visit the sick.

"The Holy One, blessed be He, buried the dead, as it is written, *And He buried him in the valley in the land of Moab.*[14] Do likewise: bury the dead.

"The Holy One, blessed be He, comforted those who mourned, as it is written, *And it came to pass after the death of Abraham, that God blessed Isaac his son.*[15] Do likewise: comfort those who mourn."[16]

THE MEANING OF COMPASSION

God enters the life of man in compassion. When man opens his hard heart and receives the bounty of God's love, which streams toward him unceasingly as the rays of the sun, seeking again and again to enter, he cannot use this love simply to fill the void of his own soul, nor is it sufficient to express it in prayer. Something more is demanded. For hidden in God's love for one man is God's love for all men. The man who feels God's love for him, feels also God's love for other men, and he too participates in that love. It is this love of man for his fellow

194

man, which is God's love for all men, that we call compassion.

"It must be clear to us," wrote Rabbi Nahum of Tchernobil, "that human love is but the consequence of divine love, since without divine love no love could be aroused from our heart." The Baal Shem asked every man to consider: "What is it which stirs within me imitations of love, if not the love of God for His creation?"

We love with the love wherewith we are loved.

But what does compassion, our love for our fellowman, mean?

Compassion means, first of all, the recognition of the existence of others, the realization that there are other people who have the same desires, dreams, weaknesses and pains as we. The blinders of pride, which turn our eyes inward upon our own ego and prevent us from seeing those who are round about us, are stripped from our souls at the moment of compassion.

Compassion means more, however, than mere recognition of our neighbor. It is an attitude toward him, a going out of ourselves toward him, to meet him, to embrace him, to love him. Am I my brother's keeper? was Cain's question. The implicit answer is "Yes, you are your brother's keeper." One of the first lessons in the Bible, then, is that every man is your brother and you are his keeper; you are responsible for him, for his joy, his sadness, for his success, his failure. All men are somehow bound together in an eternal bond of life and death.

Thou shalt love thy neighbor as thyself is the classic statement of the Bible. But how do we love our neighbor? Rabbi Moshe Leib of Sassov, by relating an experience in his life, tells us.

"How to love men is something I learned from a peasant. He was sitting in an inn along with the other peasants, drinking. For a long time he was as silent as all the rest, but when he was moved by the wine, he asked one of the men seated beside him in a voice unsteadied by drink: 'Tell me do you love me or don't you love me?' The other, also with a clumsy tongue, replied, 'I love you very much.' But the first peasant nodded his head, was silent for a while, then remarked: 'You say that you love me, but you do not know what I need. If you really loved me, you should know.' The other had not a word to say to this, and the peasant who had put the question fell again silent. But I understood. *'To know the needs of men and to bear the burden of their sorrow—that is the true love of man.'* "

This then is the deepest meaning of compassion. To know the needs of men and to bear the burden of their sorrow is the most profound way in which we love our neighbor. By knowing his needs, by feeling his pain, by sharing his anguish, by bearing the burden of his sorrow, we pour forth from our heart the love which God extends to us.

In a memorable Midrash a procession of the leaders of ancient Israel from Abraham to Jeremiah appear before the Lord, each one recounting his own deeds of self-sacrifice and imploring God, for their sake, to make an end to the suffering of His exiled people. But none of their pleas avail.

"Then Rachel, our mother, stood up before God and said, 'It is known to thee that Jacob, thy servant, loved me with a special love, and that he served my father because of me seven years, and when the seven years were over, and the time of my nuptials was at hand, my father determined to give my sister to my husband instead of me; and the thing appeared so dreadful to me when I learned of his plan that I revealed it to my husband, and I gave him signs that he should distinguish between me and my sister, so that my father should not be able to substitute her for me. But afterwards I repented, and I overcame my desire, and I had pity on my sister, lest she come to shame. And in the evening, when they substituted my sister for me, I entrusted to my sister all the signs which I had given to my husband, so that he might think that it was I. And not only that, I crept under the bed in which he lay with my sister, and when he spoke to her, she was silent, and I answered him throughout, so that he might not recognize my sister by her voice. And I acted lovingly towards her and I was not jealous, and did not expose her to shame. And if I, who am flesh and blood and ashes, was not jealous of my rival, and did not expose her to shame and reproach, why shouldst thou, eternal King, the loving and merciful One, be jealous of idols who have no reality in them, so that thou hast sent my children into exile, and let them be slain by the sword, and suffered their enemies to do unto them according to their pleasure?'

"Then the compassion of God was stirred and He said, 'For thy sake, Rachel, I will restore Israel to their land,' as it is said, *Thus says the Lord: A voice is heard in Ramah, lamentation and bitter weeping; Rachel weeping for her children refuses to be comforted, because they are not.*

"*Thus says the Lord, 'Refrain thy voice from weeping, and thine eyes from tears, for thy work shall be rewarded, and they shall come again from the land of the enemy.*"[17]

God's compassion waited for one who had shown compassion.

If the mother of a friend dies, it is not enough to attend the funeral or even to pay a condolence call and wear a solemn face, when this attendance and this visit and this face is but the result of what duty and propriety dictate. There is no love between such friends. If he is indeed a friend, and his mother, who bore him and raised him, who cherished him and hoped for him, has died, then something must also die in us, at least for an instant. It should cause us a touch of pain. We must feel something of the weight of that sorrow. There must be the consideration of what the death of our mother would mean to us. Only from such an understanding and sympathy can real help come.

Compassion is the pain a father feels when his son hurts his hand playing ball, the pang a mother knows when her daughter is not invited to the party she had her heart set on, the concern a lover has for the least concern of his beloved, the anguish which touches a man when his friend bares his troubles to him, the tears a child sheds for the limp foot of his dog or the broken arm of her doll, the sigh a judge heaves when he must pronounce stern sentence, the care a doctor exerts toward a patient in pain, the dull tug at the heart of a soldier when he sees the destruction he has wrought, the help a businessman extends toward a failing competitor, the forgiveness a man grants toward one who has hurt him, the pleading of Moses when the people were to be destroyed because of their golden idol, the weeping of Rachel for the exiles who trudged by her grave on the way to Babylon. Compassion is the eternal mercy of the Lord toward the folly and misery of man.

How can a man know the needs of other men and bear the burden of their sorrow?

What is there in the very nature of our being which makes it possible for fathers and mothers and lovers and friends and judges and doctors and soldiers and just ordinary people to have compassion? Our bodies are separate from each other; each has its own owner. How then can we feel our neighbor's pain? The broken arm of a friend causes physical injury only to himself. And yet we know that compassion exists and that there are persons who feel great anguish when their dear ones suffer.

Indeed, whenever the Rabbi of Sassov saw anyone's suffering, either of spirit or of body, he shared it so earnestly that the other's suffering became his own. Once someone expressed astonishment at this capacity to share in another's troubles. "What do you mean 'share'?" said the rabbi. "It is my own sorrow; how can I help but suffer it?"

Physically we may be separate and apart, but spiritually we are united through the very act of creation. When God formed us, He breathed a portion of His breath into us. Each of us has a share in that breath. Each of us is a "portion of the divine from on high." Every soul is joined to every other soul by its origin in the Creator of all souls. "No man is an island of itself," wrote John Donne. "Every man is a piece of the continent, a part of the main. . . . Any man's death diminishes me, because I am involved in mankind." For if God is immanent in man, having created us and breathed our souls into us, if our life is a part of the life of God, then each man has a share in the life of every other man, for God created all men. Therefore, in God all men meet and join hands and in the spirit of their being are brothers. Because of this unity which joins all men, we are able to feel compassion for one another, to feel the hurt of another's hurt. And the more noble our soul, the more we open our hearts to God, the more we feel our kinship with all men, the wider is our sense of compassion. Most men have abundant compassion for their children, less for their friends, hardly any for strangers, and none at all for their enemies. Yet a Jewish saint was dissatisfied with himself because he had not yet overcome the "weakness" of loving his own children more than others.

The possibility of fulfilling the commandment, *Love thy neighbor as thyself*, is only understood when we read the next phrase which follows it in the Bible, *I am the Lord*. Thus God tells us, *Thou shalt love thy neighbor as thyself* because *I am the Lord*. That is to say, because your self and his are bound up in Me; because you are not really distinct and competing beings, but together share in the one existence; because ultimately you are no "self" and he no "neighbor," but one in source and destiny; because I love you both, you shall love Me in him, as yourself. "Since the souls that are as they should be are all a part of God, and since the soul of one man and the

201

soul of his neighbor are both carved out of the same throne of Splendor, therefore, *Love thy neighbor as thyself* is meant literally, for he is as you. Since *I am the Lord* who created your soul and the soul of your neighbor, 'He is as you,' and you may love him as yourself."[18]

The truth of all truths is that every man is our brother, that we are all children of one Father, all sheep of one Shepherd, all creations of one Creator, all parts of one infinite, gracious spirit that pervades and sustains all of mankind. When we are aware of that—not necessarily in any conscious fashion, but in the intuitive style of our living—then we are no longer encased in the armor of our own ego, utterly consumed by our own cares, utterly unaware of the concerns of other, utterly unbound by the bond which joins each man to his neighbor and all men to God.

Turgenev tells of an incident which occurred to a wretched beggar.

"I was walking in the street; a beggar stopped me, a frail old man. His inflamed eyes, blue lips, rough rags, disgusting sores—Oh, how terrible poverty had disfigured him! He stretched out to me his red, swollen, filthy hand; groaned and whimpered for alms. I felt in my pockets— no purse, wallet or coin did I find. The beggar waited, and his outstretched hand twitched and trembled slightly. Embarrassed and confused, I seized his hand and pressed it. . . . 'Don't be angry at me, brother; I have nothing with me, brother.' The beggar raised his bloodshot eyes to mine. His blue lips smiled and he returned the pressure of my fingers. 'Never mind,' he stammered; 'thank you for this—this too was a gift: *you called me brother.*' "

The Rabbi of Apt, Abraham Joshua Heschel, was one of those who endeavored to penetrate into the core of love and fathom its deepest mysteries, to feel the brotherhood of man in the Fatherhood of God. Indeed, his followers did not commonly refer to him by his given name, but preferred to call him by the title of his great book, *Ohev Yisroel,* "A Lover of Israel," which words alone he permitted—no mention of his piety or his learning—to be engraved on his tombstone.

He believed that he had been in this world ten times: as a high priest, a prince, a king, an exilarch, and the like—ten different kinds of nobility. But, he said, he never learned to love mankind perfectly, and so he was sent forth time after time, until he might succeed. Then he would never return again.

To love mankind perfectly, to know the needs of our fellowmen and bear the burden of their sorrow, to partake in their suffering and share in their privation, to feel the infinite bands of God which bind all men together eternally into one man—for we are not only brothers under one Father, but all the very same brother, all the very same man, all part of one universal man—is not easy to achieve.

The road is steep and filled with the stones of ambition and envy over which we stumble and the pits of hatred and malice into which we slip. Truly, it may take many lifetimes to learn how to love mankind perfectly, and we are granted only three score years and ten. Still it is difficult to drive from our minds the thought that perhaps the Rabbi of Apt spoke not for himself alone but for all men, that all of us stand in his footsteps, and that every human being is sent into this world for one purpose—to learn to love mankind perfectly.

FORGIVENESS

It may be well to examine in some detail at least one of the ways in which compassion expresses itself in our lives. The fruits of compassion are many; but among the most precious of these is forgiveness.

The bitter brew that sometimes seethes for years within the heart of a man, fed by the acids of hate and revenge, vindictiveness and implacability, ruthlessness and rancor, can destroy that man quite as completely as cancer or typhoid. Much of the sickness which today's doctors are asked to cure is initiated by the bitterness which malice produces when it rankles in the breast of one who "has an account to settle," "an old score to pay off," who wants "to have his revenge" and "will give no quarter." In the mystery and wonder of forgiveness a healing comes over us which few drugs can effect. It is to the meaning of the Day of Atonement that we must turn to find that area in Jewish life where the element of forgiveness comes most clearly to the fore.

Once on the evening of the Day of Atonement there gathered together in the House of Study of the Zaddik, Rabbi Meir of Prymishlan, many influential men and many men learned in the Torah. They waited for him to come to say Kol Nidre; but he did not come. At last he arrived, stopped at the door, looked at the crowd and said: "See, they are all waiting for me. They think that Meir will chant Kol Nidre. Even if they stand there until morning, Meir will not chant Kol Nidre. We have been taught that Yom Kippur atones for sins between man and God, but does not atone for sins between man and man until he appeases his fellowman. Therefore, Meir wishes you first to forgive one another."

The words of the Zaddik struck their hearts like a shaft. Immediately all of them cried out one to the other, "We forgive."

But still the Zaddik remained standing in the doorway and said: "Do you think Meir is a fool? Now you forgive one another, but after this holy day has passed a man will collect his debt from his fellow down to his very pillow and blanket. Therefore, Meir wishes that he who is able to pay a debt but cannot at the moment do so should be given an extension of time, and he who is not able to pay—what would you take from him, his soul? No, you must *really* forgive one another."

There were present some wealthy men from a neighboring city and they knew full well that this applied to them. They went at once to the rabbi and said to him, "Our master, we will obey, we will obey."

Immediately, he went to the Holy Ark and said, "Lord of the world, the Jews have said we have sinned and we shall not sin in the future again, and you believe and forgive them; therefore, Meir too is compelled to believe them." Then he turned to the people. "Know well, Jews, that if you heed my words you will have a good and blessed and sweet year; but he who does not hearken to my words will discover in his own house what is stored up for him."

Afterwards he began to pray Kol Nidre.

The Day of Atonement is a day for forgiveness. In the liturgy of the "Great White Fast" God is called "He who pardons and forgives all our sins." According to tradition it was on this same day many generations ago that the Lord forgave the people of Israel for having made and worshipped the golden calf on earth at the very moment when the Ten Commandments were being given to Moses in heaven.

It is written, "the Day of Atonement atones for sins between man and God, but does not atone for sins between man and his fellow, until he appeases him."[19] But why is that so? If God forgives the sins that are committed against Him, why should He not also forgive those that are committed against one's fellow men? Perhaps it is because He wants us to follow His example, to act as He does. *He forgives us* our breaking of His Law—not observing the Sabbath, not praying regularly, not speaking the truth, not studying the Torah—*in order that we might imitate Him and forgive others. For on this day He will make atonement for you to purify you from all your sins; therefore, you be pure before the Lord:*[20] *you too should forgive.* God has compassion and forgives us in order that we might have compassion and forgive others.

And so it was, until very recent times, a deeply moving custom on the afternoon preceding the Day of Atonement to visit those whom one had offended to ask for their forgiveness, and those who had offended him to offer their forgiveness. At such times there could be seen touching acts of reconciliation between brother and brother, between old and young, between merchant and competitor, between rich and poor. This was the time to extend forgiveness, because God was to forgive them. Because God forgave them, they forgave others.

Of course, we who have lived through the catastrophes of the twentieth century holocaust know very well that forgiveness has its limits. Only a fool would think otherwise. In some modern Passover *Haggadahs* the passage, *Pour out Thy wrath upon the nations who know Thee not*,[21] was expunged by those who forgot

208

justice in the midst of an over-extended, loosely-conceived compassion. Yet what passage in the *Haggadah* had more meaning and was recited with more feeling by the Jew of Auschwitz or Warsaw than this? Simply to forgive the Nazis their crimes and erase with one noble gesture deeds which must have shocked Satan himself, would be a mockery, a scandal, a disaster. Forgiveness has its limits. There is not only compassion, there is also justice—the exacting, demanding, stern call to justice. Man must learn to pay for his transgressions. If there were nothing but forgiveness in our world, there would be no world. The criminal, the cheat, the murderer would freely ply his trade, confident that no matter what crime he committed, all would be forgiven and he would never be called to the bar of judgment. The Almighty possesses not only *midat ha-rachamim*, the quality of mercy, but also *midat ha-din*, the quality of justice. Forgiveness is not a panacea, an infallible answer to all of man's ills.

But very often forgiveness can help.

Forgiveness can help between husband and wife.

No marriage, even when the partners are deeply in love, is a simple matter, without friction or disagreement, marked only by affection, harmony and unending bliss. There are always two personalities, two egos, two minds, two childhoods, two sets of memories, feelings, desires, interests and sensibilities. Sooner or later a clash must come.

What a blessing it would be if, instead of building higher and higher walls of animosity which may one day serve to separate them altogether, a husband and wife learned to forgive one another, tried to understand how the other feels and gave a little of oneself first. God forgives us. Why? So that a husband might forgive his wife and a wife her husband. As God forgives us, we should forgive others.

Forgiveness can help between parents and children.

How many parents are turned away from their own children by the malice they feel toward their children-in-law? How many children, who thought they were treated badly by their parents many years ago, now stand trembling at freshly turned graves and shed tears of regret for not having forgiven them before?

Parents should forgive; children should forgive. The Baal Shem was once asked by a woman what she should do about her wayward son. "Love him even more," was his reply. His words are oftentimes true for sons with wayward mothers as well. The prophet says, *I shall turn the hearts of the parents to the children and the hearts of the children to the parents.*[22]

What a blessing it would be if parents and children could learn to forgive one another, could try to understand how the other person feels and give a little of himself first. God forgives us. Why? So that parents might forgive children and children might forgive parents.

We know that we *should* forgive—husbands and wives, parents and children, friends and relatives, not in every case—for there are always exceptions—but in almost every case. The question is not so much why we *should* forgive, but why we *don't* forgive? The answer to this question takes us back to the last chapter on humility, for it is in this area that the problem has its origin.

There is usually only one obstacle which prevents us from forgiving—ourselves. Our own sense of superiority and perfection, the illusions of grandeur which pride sows and arrogance reaps, blinds us to the situation of others —parents, friends, the neighbors next door or our own children. We tend to see only ourselves, to become overly sensitive and easily offended, able to hate or be jealous at the first opportunity. We think only of the self. What happens during the day is important or unimportant, remembered or forgotten, a source of joy or pain, only in relation to its effect upon us.

To forgive a word which touches the tender defenses of our ego or the phrase which casts a doubt on the pristine purity of our deeds or, for that matter, the lack of the proper word or phrase which we expect—nay, demand—is hard for most of us. Some of the greatest figures in all history, geniuses in their way and adored

211

by the world, found forgiveness a virtue they somehow could not attain. Michelangelo was among the most renowned of artists. His soul responded to all that was beautiful, his fingers created miracles of marble that all the world acclaims, his brush mirrored his fertile imagination. The paintings on the ceiling of the Sistine Chapel and his statue of Moses are works of supreme art. Yet, he could not forgive. A friend once dared to criticize one of his pictures. He never forgave him. So it was with Dante, whose magnificent poem of life and death, God and man, is one of the most remarkable and profound epics ever penned and is studied to this day in a dozen languages in all of the world's great universities. Yet he, too, found it hard to forgive. In *The Divine Comedy* he describes in self-satisfying detail the harsh punishments which will be meted out in the future world to all of his enemies and critics.

The first step on the road of forgiveness is a realization that we, too, are sinful, full of imperfection, creatures as well as creators, fallible, finite, mortal beings who err, go astray and commit transgressions. Not even a Michelangelo and a Dante were without flaw.

> What are we? What is our life? What is our goodness? What our righteousness? What our help? What is our strength? What is our might? What shall we say before Thee, O Lord our God and God of

212

> our fathers? Are not the mightiest as
> naught before Thee, and men of renown
> as though they were not, wise men as if
> they were without knowledge, and men of
> understanding as though they were lacking
> in discretion? For most of their work is
> emptiness, and the days of their lives are as
> vanity before Thee.[23]

Before God we are all imperfect.

Let a father who is angry with his son recall the troubled history of his own youth; let a wife who is impatient with her husband consider her own failings; let a friend who is offended by another examine his own actions. "Judge not your fellowman until you are in his place."[24] When we come to realize that the act which angers us at the moment and threatens to cause ugly words and bitter feelings is something we, too, have been guilty of—or, at least, could be guilty of—that our own actions, certainly our thoughts and intentions, are not all praiseworthy, then we are less apt to condemn and less apt to be offended. In the recognition of the absolute standard, God, we know that each of us has failed and none is perfect. Only then is pride broken and humility can enter.

Humility allows us to see the other person. It opens our eyes so that we begin to understand his plight, not only our own.

But it is not enough simply to tolerate our

213

neighbor, to recognize his existence and admit his predicament. That is a passive relationship at best. We must learn to find the good in him and to embrace him in love. Here it is that humility turns into compassion. We leave the narrow hallway of the self and move toward the next person with understanding, with sympathy and, even more, with love. Not only do we tolerate or understand, but we *love* parents, children, husband, wife and friend. When we learn to break a way through the wall that the ego builds around us and begin to see the good in others and draw them close to us, then can we forgive them. Jealousy is changed to understanding; hatred to affection.

God loves us; therefore, we must love others.

God forgives us; therefore, we must forgive others.

God asks us to forgive, to have compassion, but the heart is hard. The stone it has become was not the work of an hour, but of the unremitting labor of many months. And that is why the Lord chose Yom Kippur as the day above all other days, when He asks us to forgive. It is the day of fasting from sundown to sundown, a day of prayer from evening to morning and again to evening, a day of confessing our sins, of admitting our wrongs, a day when we can no longer ignore the glory of His righteousness, the splendor of His majesty, the reign of His kingdom, the power of His justice, the ineffable wonder of His presence in the world about us and in our own lives. The incomparable beauty and the undeniable truth of the words of the prayer book—God's grandeur, man's frailty—are carried to us on the wings of ancient and mysterious melody, awakening memories buried deep in our soul, of Egypt and Sinai, of Jerusalem and Babylon, of Cordova and Frankfurt, of Vilna and Warsaw, of Ger and Lubavitch, of Dachau and Auschwitz, of a kingdom of priests and a holy people, of revelation and redemption, of the unending task which is Israel's, of what it means to be a Jew.

All this is so that our hard heart might soften during that long, long period when the body is denied and the spirit nourished, when we are open to doubts about our own righteousness and begin to think of others, an openness that might not have occurred the day before or the week before. Thus it is that the majestic holiness of this Day of Days envelops, overwhelms and transforms us, until at last our armor of pride is shattered into fragments of humility, and there is awakened within us stirrings of compassion for others—for husband, wife, children, parents, friends—for all those who yearn for our love and for whose love we long.

God loves us. Shall we not love others?
God forgives us. Shall we not forgive others?

THE LAW

It is typical of the spirit of Judaism that such an issue of the heart as compassion could not be left to the mere whim of the moment. The discipline which typifies Judaism and serves, in part, to distinguish it from Christianity, acts as a tremendous fortress of understanding and insight into the fallibility of human nature, its weakness and constant openness to evil, a fortress which by its very nature has kept intact and pure the ideals of love and compassion. While Judaism realizes quite well that the unfettered free affection of the heart as it turns into deeds of love is the most sublime form of divine service, it understands also that this human heart is, alas, *human*—frail, arbitrary, unreliable, deceitful above all things, often given not all to love, but to hatred and jealousy. Therefore, the dreams of love were fixed into the practical statutes of life which have served to discipline the people, control them in hours of passion and educate their finer sensibilities. This is the meaning and purpose of that magnificent architecture we call Jewish Law, the development and application of which, initiated by the Creator Himself, has demanded the energies and abilities of the greatest of our intellects and spirits throughout countless generations in countless countries.

Among the biblical laws we find many examples of compassion.

Thou shalt not oppress the stranger, for thou knowest the soul of the stranger, seeing you were strangers in the land of Egypt.[25]

If thou see the ass of him that hateth thee lying under his burden . . . thou shalt surely help with him.[26]

Thou shalt not muzzle the ox when he treadeth out the corn.[27] It is cruel to excite the animal's desire for food and to prevent its satisfaction.

If a bird's nest chance to be before thee in the way, in any tree or on the ground, with young ones or eggs, and the mother-bird sitting upon the young or upon the eggs, thou shalt not take the dam with the young; thou shalt in any wise let the dam go, but the young thou mayest take unto thyself.[28]

Thou shalt not oppress a hired servant that is poor and needy, whether he be of thy brethren or of thy strangers that are in thy land within the gates. At his day thou shalt give him his hire, neither shall the sun go down upon it, for he is poor and setteth his heart upon it.[29]

Thou shalt not plow with an ox and an ass

together.[30] It is cruel to yoke the weaker with the stronger.

Thou shalt not wrest the judgment of the stranger, nor of the fatherless; nor take the widow's raiment to pledge: but thou shalt remember that thou wast a bondman in Egypt and the Lord thy God redeemed thee thence: therefore, I command thee to do this thing.[31]

When thou dost lend thy neighbor any manner of loan, thou shalt not go into his house to fetch his pledge. Thou shalt stand without and the man to whom thou dost lend shall bring forth the pledge without unto thee. And if he be a poor man, thou shalt not sleep with his pledge: thou shalt surely restore to him the pledge when the sun goeth down, that he may sleep in his garment, and bless thee: and it shall be righteousness unto thee before the Lord thy God.[32]

No man shall take the mill or upper millstone to pledge: for he taketh a man's life to pledge.[33] The mill consisted of two circular stones, one above the other. The removal of one would make the other useless, and so would deprive the family of its daily supply of bread.

Ye shalt not afflict any widow or fatherless child.[34]

When thou cuttest down thine harvest in thy field, and hast forgot a sheaf in the field, thou shalt not go again to fetch it: it shall be for the stranger, for the fatherless, and for the widow: that the Lord may bless thee.

When thou beatest thine olive tree, thou shalt not go over the boughs again: it shall be for the stranger, the fatherless, the widow.

When thou gatherest the grapes of the vineyard, thou shalt not glean it afterward: it shall be for the stranger, for the fatherless, and for the widow. And thou shalt remember that thou wast a slave in Egypt: therefore, I command thee to do this thing.[35]

When a man taketh a new wife, he shall not go out in the army, neither shall he be charged with any business: he shall be free at home one year, and shall cheer his wife which he hath taken.[36]

BEYOND THE LAW

The observance of the biblical injunctions as amplified a thousandfold by the rabbis of the Talmud, who were the real builders of Jewish Law as we know it today, trained a man in the right habits of living. One of the results of such discipline was the cultivation of the quality of mercy, the feeling of pity for one's fellowman, indeed, for all God's creatures. The Law reared one to know the meaning of compassion; it commanded it, required it, taught it. But discipline, in the last analysis, is not enough. "No code, no law, even the law of God, can set a pattern for all of our living."[37] In order to go into all of life, there are times when one must go beyond the Law.

We are taught in the Talmud that if a man

219

was childless—no matter how wise or full of knowledge he might be—he was not eligible for appointment to the Sanhedrin. Why? Because he would not have experienced the lessons of compassion and mercy which every father learns while raising his children. And a man without such lessons of compassion and mercy could not be trusted to interpret the Law. The Law itself requires more than the Law.

"The law," writes Maimonides in his great code, "permits that a Canaanite slave be subjected to hard labor. Nevertheless, though this is the law, the quality of kindness and the way of wisdom demand that man should show mercy and pursue justice and never weigh down, with the yoke, his servant, nor do him harm. One should give him unreservedly of every food and of every drink. The early sages used to serve their servants every dish they themselves ate and let their servants eat even before they did. As, behold, the Psalmist has said: *As the eyes of the servants unto the hand of their master, as the eyes of a maiden unto the hand of her mistress.*[38]

"Similarly shall he not abuse his servant by either unkind deed or an unkind word. The Torah has consigned the Canaanites to slavery, not to shame. Nor shall he heap loud reproach or pile anger upon him; he shall speak to him softly and listen to his pleas. And so it is clearly brought out in the case of Job's noble ways, in which he took pride: *If I did despise the*

220

cause of my manservant or of my maidservant,
when they contended with me, what then shall
I do when God riseth up? And when he re-
membereth, what shall I answer Him? Did not
He that made me in the womb make him? And
did not One fashion us in the womb.[39]

"Cruelty and arrogance are to be found only
among idolatrous pagans. But the seed of Abraham, our father, that is, the children of Israel,
upon whom the Holy One, blessed be He,
showered the blessing of the Torah, appointing
unto them righteous laws and judgments,
should be merciful unto all. Thus with reference to the qualities of the Holy One, blessed
be He, which we were commanded to emulate,
the Psalmist says, And His tender mercies are
upon all His works.[40] And all those who show
mercy will have mercy shown unto them, as it is
said, And He shall pour mercy upon thee and
shall have compassion upon thee."[41]

On the eve of the Day of Atonement, when
the time had come to chant the Kol Nidre
prayer, all the Hasidim of Rabbi Moshe Leib
of Sassov were gathered together in the House
of Prayer waiting for the rabbi. But time passed
and he did not come. They all wondered what
important matter was delaying him on this holy
day. Then one of the women of the congregation said to herself: "I guess it will be a while
before they begin and my child is alone in the

221

house. I'll just run home and look after him to make sure he hasn't awakened. I can be back in a few minutes."

She ran home and listened at the door. Everything was quiet. Softly she turned the knob and put her head into the room—and there stood the rabbi holding her child in his arms. On his way to the House of Prayer, he

had heard the child crying and had played with it and sung to it until it fell asleep.

Rabbi Moshe Leib of Sassov was a very tolerant man. Whenever he acted as a judge in a dispute he would look for any possible excuse to be lenient. Upon one occasion, the lax conduct of the community *shohet* (ritual slaughterer) gave cause for much complaint. His dis-

222

missal was demanded by all. Only one man appeared in his defense when the case was brought up before the rabbi. The good sage, his brow knitted, listened to the testimony of the witnesses. Then he announced his decision, "I absolve the *shohet* of all blame and rule that he retain his post." Thereupon a clamor arose.

"Rabbi!" cried one, "how can you take the word of one single man against the testimony of many?"

The rabbi replied gently: "When God commanded Abraham to bring his only son Isaac as a sacrifice upon His altar, did not Abraham listen then to a mere angel who stayed his hand from killing the boy? Yet God found this just, although it opposed His will. And God's reason for this is plain. To do a man harm requires a decision from high authority—to save him from harm, only a word from the most insignificant source."

Rabbi Wolf of Zbarazh had a stern sense of justice. Far and wide he was famed as an incorruptible judge. One day his own wife raised an outcry that her maid had stolen an object of great value. The servant, an orphan, tearfully denied the accusation.

"We will let the Rabbinical Court settle this!" said her mistress angrily.

When Rabbi Wolf saw his wife preparing to go to the Court, he immediately began to put on his Sabbath coat.

"Why do you do that?" she asked in surprise. "You know it is undignified for a man of your position to come to Court with me. I can very well plead my own case."

"I am sure you can," answered the rabbi. "But who will plead the case of your maid, the poor orphan? I must see that full justice is done her."

THOSE WHO LOVE US NOT

Compassion means more than love and pity and a going out of oneself toward those who are close to us, whom we understand and sympathize with. At its most sublime it means concern for those removed from us, whom we, at first, do not at all understand, and, far from sympathizing with, actually hold in contempt, even despise. The real test is not whether we have compassion upon our wife, but upon our divorced wife; not upon our child, but upon the boy with whom he quarrels; not upon our father, but upon a cantankerous uncle; not upon our employee, but upon our employer; not upon a harmless salesman, but upon a business competitor; not upon our fellow farmers, but upon the suspicious city slicker; not upon our fellow clergymen, but upon the obstreperous layman; not upon our fellow religionists, but upon the one who denies our religion; not upon fellow Americans, but upon critical foreigners; not upon our friends, but upon those we dislike and try to avoid. For if to have compassion is to imitate the Divine, then it must not be reserved for friends.

"Thou shalt walk in His ways.[42] What are His ways? Just as it is God's way to be merciful and forgiving to sinners, and to receive them in their repentance, so do you be merciful to one another. Just as God is gracious so you be gracious to one another. Just as God is long-suffering to those who transgress, so you be long-suffering to one another."[43]

Why is it that, regarding Succot, Israel is commanded in the Torah three times to rejoice, but regarding Passover not even once? Is Passover not as great a holiday as Succot? Surely, it is at least as great. If Israel had not been redeemed from Egypt, which is what Passover celebrates, they would never have been able to travel through the wilderness en route to the Promised Land, which is what Succot celebrates. Furthermore, the former is held in greater reverence than the latter and observed with far greater care and zeal. The answer is clear. At Passover many Egyptians lost their lives when the walls of the Red Sea poured down upon them, and the memory of the death of even the wicked evokes grief and not a commandment of joy. Thus, during Succot, the jubilant *Hallel* psalms are recited all eight days, but on Passover they are recited only on the first two days, for it is written, *When thine enemy falls, do not rejoice.*[44]

At the Seder table one is bidden to remove a

drop of wine from his cup at the mention of each of the ten plagues so that the cups from which one drinks might be less than full and one's joy less than complete. Indeed, the Lord silenced even the very angels in heaven who were singing over the victory of the Israelites at the Red Sea: "Will you dare to rejoice when my creatures are dying?"[45]

In later centuries, too, the lives of the Jewish saints were luminous with this kind of sympathy.

One midnight when Rabbi Moshe Leib of Sassov was absorbed in the mystic teachings, he heard a knocking at the window. A drunken peasant stood outside and asked to be let in and given a bed for the night. For a moment the Zaddik's heart was full of anger, and he said to himself, "How can a drunk have the insolence to ask to be let in, and what business has he in this house?"

But then he said silently in his heart: "And what business has he in God's world? But if God gets along with him, can I reject him?"

He opened the door at once, and prepared a bed.

When Rabbi Moshe Leib of Sassov died he said to himself: "Now I am free from fulfilling the commandments. What can I do now that will be in obedience to the will of God?" He thought for a while. "It must surely be God's

will that I be punished for my countless sins!"
And immediately he began to run with all his
might and jumped straight into hell. Heaven
was very much perturbed at this, and soon the
prince of hell was told not to stoke his fires
while the Rabbi of Sassov was down there.
Thereupon the prince begged the Zaddik to
take himself off to paradise, for this was clearly
not the place for him. It just would not do to
call a holiday in hell for his sake.

"If that is the case," said the Moshe Leib,
"I won't stir from here until all the souls that
are imprisoned here are allowed to go with me.
On earth I made it my business to ransom
prisoners, and so I certainly will not let these
unfortunates suffer in this prison."

And they say that he had his way.

Rabbi Shmuel of Nikolsburg was once asked
how it is possible to love a man who does evil
to him. He answered that we are told to love
our fellowman as ourselves. For example, if
you unintentionally strike your own body with
your hand or foot, you would certainly not grow
angry at your hand or foot. Likewise we must
love our fellowman and not hate him even
though he hurts us, as if he were indeed one of
our own limbs.

Said the Rabbi of Radomsk: "It is often
asked why the present exile of Israel lasts so
long. One reason may be that the Shekhinah,

227

which is also in exile, is impatient to return to the Holy Land and desires that the good Jews be redeemed, even if the impious ones assimilate and lose their faith. But the Zaddikim have compassion on the irreligious also, and petition the Lord to grant them a longer time wherein to strive for the repentance of the impious, so that they also may be redeemed.

A number of Zaddikim met in Levov and discussed the corrupt ways of the new generation. There were many who were giving up the holy customs, wearing shorter robes, cutting their beards and sidelocks, and would soon backslide spiritually as well. They thought it imperative to do something to stop the stones from crumbling or else—on a day not too far off—the entire lofty structure would collapse. And so those who had met to confer on this matter resolved to set up solid bounds and to make a beginning by forbidding renegades to appeal to the court of arbitration. But they agreed not to make this decision effective until they had the consent of Rabbi Wolf of Zbarazh. Several Zaddikim reported to him the results of the meeting and made their request.

"Do you think I love you more than them?" he asked.

The decision was never put into effect.

The shepherds of Israel, throughout the ages, were men who displayed compassion for their people in their time of trouble. Because Moses left his royal station and defended the Hebrew slave whom the Egyptian taskmaster was beating and, later, when tending the flocks on the lonely slopes of Midian, caught up a helpless, injured lamb and held it to his breast, he was considered worthy of leadership. So it was with Hosea when he forgave a wife who had been wantonly unfaithful to him. So it is with every true leader of a people. Thus the words of Scripture, *But Abraham still stood before the Lord*,[46] were interpreted to mean that Abraham and his successors, the leaders of each generation, still stand before the Lord to implore compassion for sinners, as Abraham did on behalf of Sodom.

COMPASSION AND THE
JEWISH PEOPLE

Compassion, however, was not only for saints, for the exalted few in Jewish life. It expressed itself as well in the life of the people and grew into institutions of daily life that a person participated in, not because of any unusual qualities he might possess, but simply because he was a Jew and that was the way Jews lived.

What Jewish community did not possess a *Bikkur Holim* Society to provide medical expenses for the sick who could not depend on their families to pay for doctor or drugs, and to visit the ill and bring them cheer, comfort and financial help in their plight; a *Malbish Arumim* Society to clothe the poor; a *Hachnosat Kalah* Society to dower the needy bride; a *Bet Yetomim* Society to subsidize the orphanage; a *Talmud Torah* Organization to support a free school for orphans and needy children; a *Gemillat Hesed* Society to lend money at no interest to those in privation; an *Ozer Dalim* Society to dispense charity to the poor who were too proud to go from door to door and

ask for it; a *Hachnosat Orchim* Society to give
shelter to the homeless traveler; a *Linat Zedek*
Society to provide someone to stay in the room
where the dead lay; a *Hevrah Kaddishah* to
attend to the burial of the dead and care for
the personal needs of the mourners, allowing
the family, prostrated with grief, to mourn the
deceased and not worry about practical matters;
a *Ma'ot Chittim* Society to make it possible for
even the neediest to have unleavened bread
and all else that was necessary to observe the
Passover. Poor students were fed daily in the
homes of the community. This too became a
kind of institution and had a special name,
essen teg.

It was considered improper not to have a
stranger at the Sabbath table each Friday night.
To share one's bedroom with the homeless or
the traveler was the least one could do. Women
often took time from their work to help the
sick and care for their children. Frequently they
would bake more than they needed in order to
distribute the rest to the poor; or, when preparing a trousseau for their daughters, they
would set aside a piece of linen for a poor Jewish bride for each one they used for their own
child. No house was so poor that it did not
possess small tin boxes into which coins were
dropped to support various good causes. Each
Friday afternoon at sunset, before lighting the
Sabbath candles, the housewife would regularly
put money into one or more of these boxes.

Children, too, were trained in the habit of giving and often were the ones designated to place the coin in a poor beggar's hand when he made his way from door to door.

"The degree of destitution among the Jews was enormous at the time when ghetto deprivation was at its height; it is computed, for example, that in the eighteenth century one in three of the Jewish population in Germany, England and Italy, was dependent upon his coreligionists for relief, and as many more were living upon the border-line of penury. Yet the cry for assistance was never made in vain; and relief was given in such a manner as to facilitate the maximum of self-reliance, and to avoid pauperization.

"It was realized from the beginning that the poor have rights, and the rich have duties; and this, explicitly laid down in the Mosaic code, was extended and crystallized in talmudic practice. From the period of the fall of the Jewish state, the charity overseer was part of the recognized institutional system of every community. It was expected of the medieval Jew that he should devote a tithe of his income, at the very least, to philanthropic objects: and this ideal has been preserved to our own day. Even the pauper, who lived on the charity of others, was expected to contribute his mite to the relief of those more needy than himself.

"Every ghetto had its Lodging House for indigent strangers, which was also used as a

232

hospital; every community had its salaried physician, so that medical attendance was available for all. There was, too, a free educational system, supported by voluntary subscriptions and open to every child. A town without its proper charity organizations, it was laid down in the codes, was no proper residence for self-respecting Jews, any more than if it lacked its place of worship. Yet at the same time, it was established as a cardinal principle, that the poor should not be put to shame by the method of administering relief. As early as the fourth century, the Emperor Julian, when he ordered the institution of inns for strangers in every city, referred with admiration to the example of the Jews, 'the enemies of the gods,' in whose midst no beggars were to be found.

"It should be noted though, in this connection, how catholic was the Jewish conception of charity. It is a man's duty, we are informed in the Talmud, to relieve the Gentile poor, and to visit their sick, and to bury their dead, just as though a co-religionist were in question. This principle was not inculcated for the sake of appearances or of policy, but on a purely ethical basis, being deduced from the verse of the Psalm which tells how the tender mercy of the Lord is *over all* His creatures. . . . It is illuminating to compare this with the spectacle which horrified the world at the time of the expulsion from Spain in 1492, when zealous friars wandered on the quay-side in Genoa, loaves of bread in one hand and a crucifix in the other, offering food in return for a recognition of the spiritual pre-eminence of Christianity."[47]

Mercy was not only shown to one's fellowman, be he Jew or Gentile, but to all living things: the beasts of the field, the fish of the sea and the birds of the air. We are taught not to harm a single living thing, not a fly or an ant, not even a spider. For they too are God's creatures. And these too suffer when they are hurt. Thus while we recite a benediction when first putting on any manner of new clothing, there is one exception to this law. No benediction is to be made over shoes, because they are made of leather, and an animal must be killed to obtain it. The eating of meat presented a great problem to our people. It would not be difficult to present a strong case, from Jewish sources, for vegetarianism. Adam, for example, the ideal man, lived on fruits and vegetables. Meat was only permitted to be eaten under certain conditions: that the blood be removed and that the animal be slaughtered with the very least amount of pain by a skilled and pious person who understood the seriousness of his task. Thus *zaar baal hayyim* (cruelty to anything possessed of life) was a crime. "The slaughter of beasts for food was hedged by the most elaborate precautions to minimize, if not to suppress, pain completely. To eat a 'limb of the living animal' was regarded as a mark of

234

barbarism: today eels are still skinned alive, cod is crimped and lobsters are boiled unpithed. It is remarkable that Jews did not kill animals for sport. Fish had to be netted. Mr. William Radcliffe, in his book, *Fishing from the Earliest Times* (London, 1921), blames Jews for lacking the sporting spirit. They caught fish by net, they did not play them with the rod. This is perfectly true. The work 'hook' occurs in the Bible only as a metaphor of cruelty, or as an instrument used by foreigners."[48] Animals as well as humans are God's creatures, and toward all of God's creatures we are taught to show mercy.

Knowing the needs of others and feeling their suffering is the meaning of compassion. It is a meaning not unknown to the life of the Jewish people.

It was otherwise among the pagans. Compassion was not of great consequence in their lives. They did not praise it or teach it. It was not accounted as one of the chief virtues, a way in which man could become like unto God himself. One looks for it in vain in Homer; nor is its absence much noted. In the *Iliad* it is dispassionately described as a quality "which greatly injures and also greatly benefits men."[49] Plato does not bother to treat it in any detail, characteristically noting, however, that the "ignorant" man is more to be pitied than the "suffering" one.[50] Aristotle gives it somewhat more attention, not because it is a vital human

235

virtue, but because it is important for rhetorical purposes.[51] The Stoics considered it a weakness which the "wise man" should seek to rid himself of. Indeed, one must look long and hard through the Latin writers to find passages which display any understanding of the quality of mercy or compassion or pity. Peoples who could leave old men to die, forsake deformed children on mountain tops, who could recline comfortably in great amphitheaters and impassively watch the "sport" of human beings torn apart by beasts of the jungle, were not easily given to feelings of pity or compassion. There was something lacking in their society which has always been present in ours. What was lacking was the tradition of the Bible; what was lacking was the teaching of a God of compassion who looked down upon the humble and had pity on the orphan and the widow, who listened to the prayers of the sick and hearkened to the cry of the humiliated, who drew close to the broken-hearted and did not abandon the old, who suffered with those in pain and went into exile along with His people— the teaching which over the centuries built a way of life among Israel in which compassion was a cornerstone and mercy the other side of every act of justice, in which there lived a Baal Shem and a Rabbi of Sassov whose exalted lives thousands of simple men and women learned from and tried to imitate.

We cannot, of course, all live on the spiritual

236

heights of the Baal Shem or the Rabbi of Sassov, but compassion can become an attitude when God enters our lives. An ancient rabbi spoke wiser than he knew when he said that the Jew who has no pity, no compassion for his fellow man, is not of the seed of Abraham, but of the mixed multitude which came out of Egypt with Israel and did not stand at Mount Sinai. Even their justice was tempered by mercy. The people of Israel have been known throughout the ages as a people of compassion. They are called *Rachamanim*, *b'nei Rachamanim*, "compassionate ones, and the children of the compassionate ones." We are taught that the holy and awesome name of the Lord, YHWH, which remains secret and unpronounced, signifies compassion. What a world of meaning there is in the Yiddish word, *rachmonus*, and what a role it played in the Yiddish language. It is not an exaggeration to say that one of the few remaining distinctively Jewish traits, despite rapid assimilation in the postemancipation world, is compassion. To some extent it is still felt. It has become embedded too deeply in the lives of the people to be lost in a few generations. Jews do respond to charitable needs more quickly than many others; Jews do go out of their way for the sake of the sick, the hungry, the helpless, more than is their rightful obligation. It is common knowledge that Jews are leaders in endeavors which seek to alleviate suffering and raise the

237

lot of mankind. Some say we are a softhearted people. If this be true, then God forbid that we lose that soft heart. It is one of the rarest and dearest of possessions in a pagan century, outstanding in its lack of compassion.

But will the present generation of the children of Israel be able to maintain this burning sense of compassion which characterized their ancestors, and, even more important, will they be able to perpetuate it in the lives of their children? This is the question which demands an answer. The answer is not easy to give.

The hardness of our time has left its mark on all of us and the frigid winds of the modern world have enveloped us in a cloud of ambition and acquisition, have blown us far from the rich soil of spiritual living that nourished us over the centuries, into an arid tract where the earth must once again be tilled and where the strength for tilling is weak.

The compassion which we still show is largely an inheritance from parents more pious than we, an attitude with which we grew up and accepted naturally. But while to the past generations compassion followed strongly from the very presence of the Divine in their lives, which prayer, Torah-study and observance of the commandments renewed daily, to most of us, their children and grandchildren, it follows weakly from habit that loses vigor with the passage of time. For the past generations it was the deeply sunken spring of the spirit that, reaching down

238

into the Source of all springs, gave forth the sweet waters of mercy. For us the taste is still present in our mouths; we even use it occasionally to nourish the land around us; but the spring is hardly ours any longer. And for how long will we be able to draw water from it when it begins to dry up? It is only God's presence in our lives which assures us of the wonder of forgiving, the joy of pity, the marvel of love.

The prayer of God Himself is a prayer for compassion: "May it be My will that My compassion might overcome Mine anger and prevail over My justice, that I might deal with My children according to the attribute of compassion."[52]

May this, too, be our prayer.

EPILOGUE

Prayer, humility and compassion, these are three ways in which God enters the life of man. In terms of man's relation to heaven, He enters our lives in prayer; in terms of man's relation to himself, in humility; in terms of man's relation to his fellow man, in compassion. They are not three lonely paths, each leading to a dead end. They are connected one with the other. They interact constantly. For at the root of them all is God's love for man.

When God enters our lives, we are overwhelmed by the stream of His love; and our self-love, which is pride, gives way, making room for love of God, which is prayer. Yet our love for God, caused by the steady flow of God's love for us which we return, cannot be contained in the silver cup of prayer and so pours over into love for our fellow man, which is compassion.

But the ways of the Lord are often hidden ways. Whether the road to compassion is through prayer and humility or, perhaps, the reverse, cannot be foreseen. A moment of prayer at a time of grief may break the proud heart of a man. An unselfish act of love may take a man so out of himself that prayer will become possible. At what point God's love enters a man's life and the course it may follow cannot be predicted, but of nothing are we more certain than that it is continuously trying to break in upon us.

His love for us is like the rays of the sun which pass through a prism and are broken into a spectrum of different colors. We do not see the sun's rays themselves in these colors, but we know that the colors are due to them. Similarly, God pours forth his love upon us. We are the prism which refracts his rays of love into the many colors of our virtues, among which are prayer, humility and compassion. And just as the brightness of the sun can no longer be discerned in the colored rays, but is surely their source and cause, so the Lord cannot be seen in our prayer, our modesty, our compassion, yet these are within us only because of Him.

The drama of a life intertwined with the life of God, receiving His love, sharing it and bestowing it upon others, is surely the most profound action of human existence. But for that love to enter us at all, we must first raise the many heavy barriers to our heart that we have so carefully erected through the years and open the doors of the spirit that we have locked to obstruct His entrance.

241

This is why Rabbi Baruch, the grandson of the Baal Shem, when once reading the Psalms as was his custom each day, was so deeply stirred by the words, *I will not give sleep to mine eyes, nor slumber to mine eyelids until I find out a place for the Lord.*[53] He stopped and recast it for himself, "Until I find *myself* and make *myself* a place to be ready for the descent of the Divine Presence."

Really to find ourselves means that we must make ourselves a place where God will dwell, a tabernacle of flesh and blood for the Spirit of all spirits to reside in.

It is as if there were once a man who, after many years, was blessed with an only child, who was therefore very dear to him and for whom he made great plans and set grand goals. Upon him he lavished all his affection, raising him with love, guiding him through youthful years, educating him with care in the ways of life, helping him in times of doubt, even preparing for him a detailed blueprint of how he might most easily reach those goals. And always, during all those years, the father tried to remain at the side of his beloved son with whom he made his home, for the father was alone in the world and hoped to dwell with his son. So it was, when the son was exiled from his native land and had to wander in strange countries, suffering hardship and privation, that the father drew even closer to him in love and pity. But then the son found security and prosperity in a new and rich land and in the achievements of his own mind. He forgot his father and all that he had done for him and all that he still hoped for him. He forgot that his father was still hoping to be with him once again. . . .

But, in truth, both father and son needed one another. The father needed his son to fulfill his dreams and to offer a home. The son needed his father to be reminded what those dreams were.

So it is with us. God is our loving father and we are his beloved child. He has fashioned us in His own image, redeemed us from slavery, guided us through the wilderness, watched over us wherever our path has led, chosen us to be His own. He dreamed many dreams and made many plans. He gave us a picture of His vision and a replica of His plan in the Torah. All this time he tried to remain close to us, for the purpose of all creation was that we might become His dwelling-place. Most of the time it was so. Indeed, when we were driven from our land into exile, it was, in a sense, no exile at all, for the more we thought we were in exile because of our sins—far from Him and He far from us in an exile of people and God—the more we humbled ourselves, lived compassionately and prayed to Him. And the more we opened our hearts to His presence, the closer we really were to Him and the nearer He drew in love to us. But now that we have found security and success, dwell in ease and comfort, seem to live at peace with our neighbors and take pride in our achievements, we no longer consider ourselves in an exile of the spirit, but assume that our worldly success means that God in His favor sheds the light of His countenance upon us and that He surely dwells with us in our magnificent Temples and our proud hearts. We have forgotten Him and all He meant to us, confident that *our strength and the might of our hands have achieved all this*. It is the deepest truth and the most profound wisdom that in the very moment we become certain that we are not in exile, we are, indeed, in the deepest exile. For He has been driven from us, hiding His face in shame, wandering alone, away from His beloved child for whose future He had planned and dreamed.

We are thus both alone and both in need of the other.

God needs us as His abiding place so that we might fulfill His dreams.

We need God to be reminded of those dreams.

But we have even forgotten our need.

And so, He yearns again to be with us, to be close to us, to dwell in the room we could find and fashion for Him, the place we could make for Him in our hearts and souls and lives—if only we would!

But where is that place, that room?

It is our heart, our soul, our life.

He stands forlorn, abandoned, outside the windows of our days, ever peering at shades which are tightly drawn—until we act.

That is why it is best to conclude as we began.

"Where does God dwell?"
"God dwells wherever man lets Him in."

NOTES

PROLOGUE

1. Francis Thompson, "The Hound of Heaven."
2. Abraham J. Heschel, *Man Is Not Alone*, New York: JPS, and Farrar, Straus & Young, 1951, p. 244.

PRAYER

1. A. J. Heschel, *Man's Quest for God*, New York: Charles Scribner's Sons, 1954, p. 6.
2. *Ibid.*, p. 7.
3. From the Holy Day Liturgy.
4. Genesis 18.27.
5. *Otzar Tefillah*, p. 114.
6. Heschel, *op. cit.*, p. 61.
7. *Ibid.*
8. 1 Kings 19.11-13.
9. Heschel, *Man Is Not Alone*, p. 128.
10. Heschel, *Man's Quest for God*, p. 15.
11. Deuteronomy 7.6.
12. Max Heiler, *Prayer*, New York: Oxford University Press, 1934, p. 353.
13. Sanhedrin 22a.
14. Psalm 139.3-4, 7-12.
15. Chagigah 12b.
16. From the daily liturgy.
17. From the daily liturgy.
18. *Megillot*, May, 1953, p. 66. Quoted by L. Jacobs, *Jewish Prayer*, London, 1955, p. 31.
19. Heschel, *God in Search of Man*, New York: JPS, and Farrar, Straus & Cudahy, 1955, p. 49.
20. Psalm 104.

247

21. Palestinian Talmud, Sotah 20c.
22. Psalm 73.25,27.
23. Heschel, *Man Is Not Alone*, p. 152.
24. Psalm 42.2-3.
25. Psalm 63.2-4.
26. Heschel, *Man Is Not Alone*, p. 239.
27. Heiler, *op. cit.*, p. 357.
28. Numbers 24.40.
29. Psalm 61.
30. Heschel, *Man's Quest for God*, p. 10.
31. Psalm 139.23.
32. Berachot 13.
33. 1 Samuel 16.7.
34. Sanhedrin 106b.
35. *Sifre Deut.*, "Ekev," 41; Berachot 5,1; Berachot 30b; Taanit 8a; Ex. Rabba, "Beshallach," 22,3; Yebamot 105b; Pal. Tal. Berachot 4,3, f. 38a; Berachot 29b; *Pesikta K.* 158a.
36. Heschel, *Man's Quest for God*, p. 36.
37. *Midrash Tehillim*, 190b.
38. From the daily liturgy.
39. Psalm 24.1.
40. Psalm 115.16.
41. "Modernizing the Jewish Prayer Book," by Theodor Gaster in *Commentary*, April, 1954.
42. S. Morgenstern, *The Son of the Lost Son*, Philadelphia: JPS, 1946, p. 8.
43. Heschel, *Man's Quest for God*, p. 8.

HUMILITY

1. Coleridge, *The Devil's Thoughts*.
2. Sotah 4b-5a.
3. Proverbs 16.5.
4. Deuteronomy 8.11-17.
5. Deuteronomy 5.5.

6. Deuteronomy 1.1.
7. Blaise Pascal, *Pensées*, Modern Library Edition, p. 56.
8. From Job 38.
9. Job 42.6.
10. Psalm 90.
11. Isaiah 6.1-5.
12. *Guide to the Perplexed*, III, 52.

"I heard from an old man, whose image was like an angel of the Lord, a favored disciple of the Besht, Rabbi David of Mikolyov, that in our generation the curse of pride is overpowering. And the reason is because these generations are sunken low, far distant from the 'Source' as the heel is distant from the head. Therefore pride asserts itself. For this is the principle: The lower a man falls in virtue, the higher he rises in pride; for pride comes from a lack of reverence before the Lord who fills all worlds. Thus the more distant a man is from Him because of transgression, the more bold and proud of heart he is. We must ask God to help us in this matter, especially when we recite the prayer, 'O God keep my tongue from evil and my lips from speaking guile.' . . . And when we come to the words, 'Let my soul be unto all as the dust of the earth,' we must say them earnestly, with the proper *kavannah*." (Meshulam Feibush of Zevarish, *Derech Emet*)

13. Jacob Emden, *Perush al Avot* 4.4.
14. The Talmud says, "Observe how great are those who are meek in spirit before the Lord. At the time of the Temple, when one sacrificed a burnt-offering, a burnt-offering was

249

accounted to him, and when one offered a meal-offering, a meal-offering was accounted to him; but to him who was meek in spirit it was accounted as if he had offered all the sacrifices, as it is written, 'the sacrifices of the Lord are a broken spirit' " (Sotah 5b).

Rabbi Loew of Prague (the Maharal) explained this passage in the following manner: "He who is of a broken spirit humbles himself, and this is the purpose of the sacrifices. For the whole meaning of the sacrifices is to make known that the Lord is everything and that apart from Him there is nothing. Therefore sacrifices are offered to Him. Now when a man has a broken heart within him, it is as if he had offered all the sacrifices; for all the sacrifices together teach that all existence is considered as naught apart from God. Each sacrifice alone refers to one aspect of life and all of them, therefore, to all existence. When a man, who is king over all existence, is broken-hearted, then all existence is as nothing, because God is everything. Thus is the broken heart of man equal to all the sacrifices" (Netivot Olam, "Netiv ha-Anavah," chapt. 1).

15. Psalm 131.
16. Eruvim 13b.
17. Author unknown.
18. Reuven ben Zevi David, Keneset Yisrael, Warsaw, 1907, p. 145.
19. Mendel Bodek, Seder Hadorot Hechadash, Lublin, 1904, p. 19.
20. Psalm 107.8.

21. From the daily liturgy.
22. *Tanna debe Eliyahu* p. 78.
23. Erich Fromm, *Man for Himself*, New York: Rinehart and Co., p. 150,2.
24. Mishnah Sanhedrin 4,5.
25. *Deuteronomy Rabba*, "Re'eh" 4,4.
26. Mishnah Sanhedrin 4,5.
27. Genesis 18.27.
28. Numbers 12.3.
29. Exodus 32.32.
30. "Rabbi Yochanan said: 'Wherever you find mentioned in Scripture the greatness of the Holy One blessed be He, you also find mention of His gentleness. This occurs in the Torah, is repeated in the Prophets and appears a third time in the Writings. It is written in the Torah, *For the Lord your God, He is the God of gods and Lord of lords* (Deut. 10.17); and it says immediately afterwards, *He doth execute justice for the fatherless and the widow*. It is repeated in the Prophets: *For thus saith the High and Lofty One, that inhabiteth eternity, whose name is holy* (Isa. 57.15); and it is said immediately afterwards, *I dwell with him that is of contrite and humble spirit*. It is stated a third time in the Writings: *Extol Him that rideth upon the skies whose name is the Lord* (Ps. 68.5); and immediately afterwards it is written, *A father of the fatherless and a judge of the widows*'" (Megillah 31a).
31. Isaiah 66.1-2.
32. Isaiah 57.15.
33. Psalm 34.19; Zohar, Vayikra, 9a.

34. Psalm 139.8.
35. Isaiah 55.1.
36. Taanit 7a.
37. Deuteronomy 7.6-7.
38. Hullin 89b.

COMPASSION

1. Nietzsche. *The Twilight of the Gods*, p. 45, translated by A. Ludov, publisher.
2. I. Tabak, *Judaic Lore in Heine*, Baltimore: Johns Hopkins University Press, 1948, p. 198.
3. P. Friedman, *Martyrs and Fighters*, New York: Praeger, 1954, pp. 275-6.
4. Leviticus 19.17.
5. Arachin 16b.
6. Jeremiah 17.9.
7. Ezekiel 36.36.
8. Isaiah 54.7,8,10.
9. From the daily liturgy.
10. Deuteronomy 13.5.
11. Deuteronomy 4.24.
12. Genesis 3.21.
13. Genesis 18.1.
14. Deuteronomy 34.6.
15. Genesis 25.11.
16. Sotah 14a.
17. Jeremiah 31.15,16; *Lamentations Rabba*, Introduction 24.
18. Samuel Laniado, *Keli Chemdah*, quoted by Glatzer, *In Time and Eternity*, New York: Shocken, 1946, p. 146.
19. Mishnah Yoma 8.9.
20. Leviticus 16.30.
21. Jeremiah 10.25.
22. Malachi 4.6.

23. From the Holy Day and daily liturgy.
24. *Ethics of the Fathers* 2.4.
25. Exodus 23.9.
26. Exodus 23.5.
27. Deuteronomy 25.4.
28. Deuteronomy 22.6-7.
29. Deuteronomy 24.15.
30. Deuteronomy 22.10.
31. Deuteronomy 24.17-18.
32. Deuteronomy 24.10-13.
33. Deuteronomy 24.6.
34. Exodus 22.22.
35. Deuteronomy 24.19-22.
36. Deuteronomy 24.5.
37. Heschel, *Man Is Not Alone*, p. 259.
38. Psalm 132.2.
39. Job 31.13-15.
40. Psalm 145.9.
41. Deuteronomy 13.18. *Mishneh Torah*, "Hilchot Avadim" IX. Quoted in *In Time and Eternity*, p. 152.
42. Deuteronomy 28.9.
43. *Tanna debe Eliyahu*, p. 135.
44. Proverbs 24.17. *Pesikta d'R. Kahana*, 189a.
45. Megillah 10b.
46. Genesis 18.22.
47. Roth, Cecil, *Jewish Contribution to Civilisation*, London, 1945, p. 288.
48. Montefiore, C., Lowe, H., *A Rabbinic Anthology*, London, 1938, p. xcii.
49. Iliad XXIV, 45.
50. Republic 539a.
51. Rhetoric II.
52. Berachot 7a.
53. Psalm 132.4.

ACKNOWLEDGMENTS

I wish to express my appreciation to the editors of the periodicals *Judaism*, *Conservative Judaism* and the *National Jewish Monthly* for permission to use material first published there, and to Schocken Books Inc. for allowing me to use their translations of certain prayers and parables. I am indebted to Dr. Maurice Friedman for his generous advice; to Rabbis Seymour Siegel and Wolf Kelman for their suggestions; to Rabbis Jack Riemer, Fritz Rothschild and Felix Levy and to Professor Abraham J. Heschel for having read the manuscript with care and offered me constant help and guidance.